iLLUSTRATiON BOOK PRO 01

イラストレーション ブック プロ 01

今、欲しいイラストが見つかる、レンタルもオーダーもできる
「使いたい、使える」ポートフォリオ

Edited by pict

イラストレーションエージェンシー・ピクト編

Foreword:

Erik Kessels

Creative Director
KesselsKramer

Profile

Erik Kessels (1966) is Creative Director of Amsterdam based communication agency KesselsKramer,
working for national and international clients such as Diesel, Oxfam, Ben and The Hans Brinker Budget
Hotel. He is a photography collector and has published several books of his collected images and is
editor of the alternative photography magazine Useful Photography. He has curated exhibitions such
as Dutch Delight at Foam (Amsterdam) and Loving Your Pictures at the Centraal Museum (Utrecht).
Kessels has taught communication at the Hallo Academy Amsterdam and photography at the Gerrit
Rietveld Academy in Amsterdam.

2kilo of KesselsKramer

Publishing Company:PIEBOOKS
257mm×148mm 880Pages(Full Color)Softbound 978-4-89444-431-7

Brick or Book? Weighing in at a staggering two kilograms the contents include;
Everything the renowned agency has made in advertising, design, music videos,
documentaries, product design,publishing and more; Go to the gym, then try and
lift 2kilo. It's the best way to see how this small agency from Amsterdam became
a heavyweight in the world of communication.

It's refreshing to see that there is a growing community of young illustrators that use their hands and brains again. In the early 90's, during the rise of Photoshop and Illustrator, illustrators leapt at the chance to use the computer as their starting point. They were almost intimidated by the abilities of this machine. Soon though, after the excitement of its initial possibilities, the realization came back again that a computer could always lend a hand in execution, but never be a starting point for a drawing. Rather, it's the idea and the translation of this idea that leads to a successful illustration. Even more than photography, illustration is an extremely personal way to put someone's thoughts on a surface. No two illustrations will ever be the same.

So after years of stiff and cold computerized work we catch the return of handiwork and craftsmanship.The revival of getting your hands dirty again. Illustrators are now rightfully acknowledged as ideas-people that should be consulted in an early stage of a briefing. In some examples, which can be seen in our '2 kilo' book, illustration is more than a drawing on paper-instead it becomes a prominent piece of the communication. One that is necessary for the strategy and concept to attain clarity and life.

As an art-director I never try to find an illustrator that can copy the ideas I have in mind. Together you work towards an end result and the illustrator should always be leading in this process. He or she is the artist and has the talent. With that in mind I try always to leave as much freedom as possible for the talent you work with. Some art-directors might have difficulties with this because an illustrator is less controllable than for instance a photographer. I find this uncontrollable factor in illustration one of the most exiting elements. Some very simple illustrations, like the work of Saul Steinberg, say more than a thousand words. Every artist has it's own handwriting, however, so it's always a matter of taste connecting somebody to a piece of communication.

Another remarkable development is the fact that illustration nowadays crosses over with a lot of other disciplines. A single piece of work is recognized as art, is shown in a gallery and used for a commercial purpose. For a long time there was a whole population of illustrators that worked only commercially and never did any autonomous work. Illustrators nowadays become artists and artists become illustrators. There are not a lot of borders anymore. Is Rita Ackerman an artist or an illustrator? Is Thomas Demand a photographer, a sculptor or an illustrator? Do you value the work of Raymond Pettibon as art or as illustration? And in the end, does it matter?

Finally, I'd like to return to the point I made at the start there's only one criterion for me. There should be an idea in every piece of artwork, same way that there should be an idea in every piece of communication. An illustration without an idea is like a body without a soul.

Erik Kessels
Creative Director
KesselsKramer

序文：

ケッセルスクライマー：クリエイティブ ディレクター
エリック・ケッセルス

プロフィール

1966年生まれ。Diesel, Oxfam, Ben やThe Hans Brinker Budget Hotelなどオランダ国内外の大手企業をクライアントに持つ、アムステルダムにあるコミュニケーションエージェンシー、KesselsKramerのクリエイティブディレクター。写真の収集家でもあり、集めた写真を出版している。オルタナティブ写真雑誌、Useful Photography誌では編集も担当。アムステルダム写真美術館（Foam）でDutch Delight、セントラルミュージアム(ユトレヒト)でLoving Your Picturesなど展示会・展覧会も主催。またアムステルダムのデザイン学校（Hallo Academy Amsterdam and photography at the Gerrit Rietveld Academy）でコミュニケーション論を教鞭。

ケッセルスクライマーの2キロ
発売元：ピエ・ブックス
257mm×148mm 880Pages(Full Color) Softbound 978-4-89444-431-7

ヨーロッパで大評判のケッセルスクライマーの作品とその秘訣を大公開！よろめくほど重い2キロのコンテンツ。広告・デザイン・ミュージックビデオ・プロダクトデザイン・出版…これを読めば、アムステルダムの小さなクリエイティブ集団がコミュニケーションの世界でヘビー級になった理由がわかる。ジムに通って、ケッセルスクライマーの2キロを持ち上げてみよう！

自分の技術と頭を使う若いイラストレーター達が台頭するのは、見ていて爽快な気持ちになる。1990年代の初め、PhotoshopとIllustratorが広まってきた時代に、イラストレーター達は取っ掛かりとしてコンピュータを使うことに飛びついた。彼らは、この機械の性能にほとんど怖気づいたものだが、コンピュータの当初の可能性に対する興奮を経験して間もなく、コンピュータは常に何かするときの手助けはしてくれるが、描くことそのものの出発点には決してなり得ないということが解ったのである。むしろ、素晴らしいイラストレーションを導くのは、アイデアであり、あるいはそのアイデアの変換である。イラストレーションは、写真よりももっとその人の考えを紙面の上に置き換える究極の個人的な方法である。全く同じイラストレーションは決して存在しないのだ。

　堅苦しく、無味乾燥としたコンピュータ化された仕事に長年携わった後、私たちは手仕事や職人芸の価値を解るものなのだ。あなたの手が再び汚れてくることの復活なのだ。イラストレーター達は今、何かを説明しようとするときにまず最初に相談すべきアイデアマンとして周囲から正しく認識されている。その幾つかの例は、私たちの著書『2キロ』の中に見ることができる。イラストレーションは、「紙の上に描かれたもの」以上の存在であり、むしろコミュニケーションの傑出した一片になっている。イラストレーションは、物事をはっきりと見えるようにし、生命を吹き込むための戦略やコンセプトのために不可欠なものなのである。

　私は、アート・ディレクターとして、自分が心の中に持っているアイデアをコピーできるイラストレーターを見つけようなどと思ったことは一度もない。最終ゴールに向けてあなたがイラストレーターと一緒に仕事をする時、そのイラストレーターは常にそのプロセスにおいてリーダーでなければならない。彼（彼女）はアーティストであり、才能を持っているのだ。このことを念頭において、私は一緒に働くイラストレーターにできる限りの自由を与えるように努力している。幾人かのアート・

ディレクターは、そのように振舞うことが難しかったかも知れない。何故なら、イラストレーターというものは例えば写真家よりももっとコントロールすることが難しい人間であるからだ。私は、世の中に存在する物の中でイラストレーションが最もコントロール不能なものの一つであると思う。ソール・スタインバーグの作品のような極めてシンプルなイラストレーションは、何万の言葉より多くを語りかける。どのアーティストも自分ならではイラストレーションを持っている。しかし、それは常に、人をコミュニケーションと結びつける好みの問題である。

　もう一つの特筆すべきことは、現代のイラストレーションが他のたくさんの分野とクロス・オーバーしてきているという事実だ。ちょっとした作品でもアートとして認められ、ギャラリーに展示され、商業目的に使用される。長年の間、商業目的以外で働くイラストレーターは皆無であり、商業目的から自立した作品を制作することも皆無であった。今日では、イラストレーターはアーティストとなり、アーティストはイラストレーターになる。そこにはもはや大きな境界線は存在しないのだ。リタ・アッカーマンはアーティストなのかイラストレーターなのか。トーマス・デマンドは写真家なのか、彫刻家なのか、イラストレーターなのか。レイモンド・ペティボンの作品をあなたはアートと見るか、イラストレーションと見るか。そして最終的には、そんなことはどうでもいいのではないか。

　最後に、私が冒頭で述べた問題に戻りたい。それこそが私にとっては唯一の判断基準なのだ。どのアート作品も、アイデアを持っていなければならない。同じように、どのコミュニケーションもアイデアを持っていなければならない。アイデアなしのイラストレーションは、魂のない肉体のようなものだから。

エリック・ケッセルス
クリエイティブ ディレクター
ケッセルスクライマー

Illustrator index イラストレーター・インデックス

Editorial note エディトリアルノート

Credit format クレジットフォーマット

A Illustrator's name イラストレーター名

B Media 画材

C What is the most important thing in your creations? 作品を創作する上で大切にしていること

D Web site address ウェブサイトアドレス

E Stock illustration number ストックイラスト番号

　　*詳細は310ページ、「ピクトのシステム」をご参照下さい。 See 310 page "System of PICT" for details.

Kyoko Aoyama
青山 京子

Enjoy!

楽しい!

Media : Photoshop5.5
画材 : Photoshop5.5

神奈川県生まれ / 東京在住 / 武蔵野美術短期大学芸能デザイン科卒

See more artwork（バリエーションはこちら）≫ http://www.pict-web.com/kyoko_aoyama

054

055

056

057

058

059

あ

011

Takao Aoyama
青山 たか生

Media : Acrylic / Oil pastel
画材：アクリル / オイルパステル

I left Waseda University midway through my studies. I have been working as a freelance illustrator since I left an advertising agency in 2003. I draw pictures in which I hope to express emotions, and the interior of characters.

早稲田大学中退後、広告制作会社を経て2003年よりフリーのイラストレーターとして活動。人物の内面、感情を表現したいと思い絵を描いています。

1974年埼玉県生まれ / 埼玉県在住 / 早稲田大学教育学部中退

See more artwork（バリエーションはこちら）≫ http://www.pict-web.com/takao_aoyama

001

002

003

004

005

006

Kenji Asazuma
浅妻 健司

Media : Pencil / Mechanical pencil / Pen /
Photoshop CS2
画材：鉛筆 / シャープペンシル / ペン /
Photoshop CS2

I want to make works with a warm and nostalgic
atmosphere. I treasure slow and easygoing time
that flows by, gestures, and countenance.

暖かく懐かしい雰囲気の作品を作っていきたいと考えてい
ます。ゆったりのんびり流れる時間や、仕草や表情を大事
にしています。

1974年横浜生まれ / 横浜在住 / セツ・モードセミナー卒

See more artwork（バリエーションはこちら）≫ http://www.pict-web.com/kenji_asazuma

001

002

003

004

005

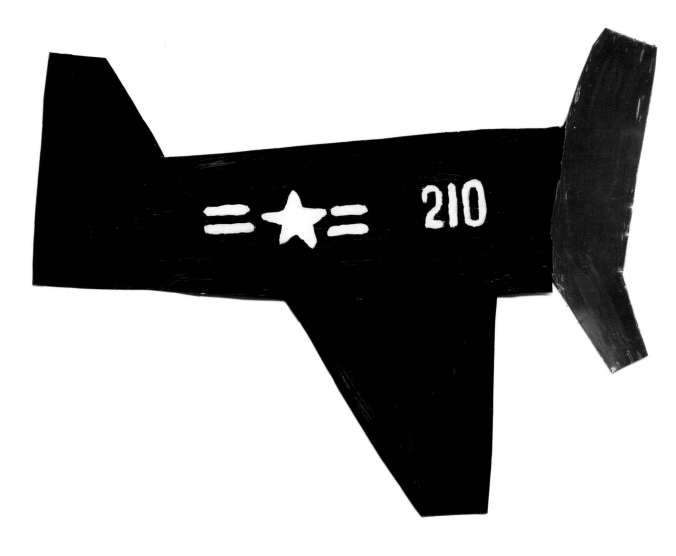

Azumimushi
あずみ虫

I'm conscious of the appeal of form. The character of my work is subtly three dimensional because I cut metal plates and draw on them.

フォルムの面白さを意識しています。金属版を切って、その上に描いているので、微妙な立体感が出るところが特徴です。

Media : Aluminum / Acrylic
画材：金属板（アルミ）/ アクリル絵具

1975年神奈川県生まれ / コム・イラストレーターズ・スタジオ卒

あ

See more artwork（バリエーションはこちら）≫ http://www.pict-web.com/azumimushi

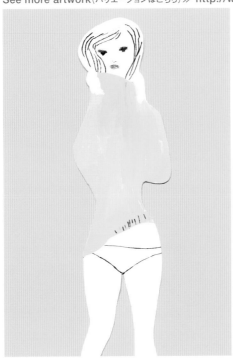

001

002

003

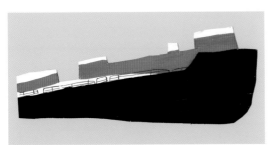

004

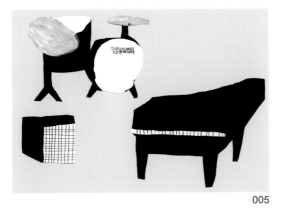

005

006

Mizuki Abe
阿部 瑞季

Media : Painter Classic
画材 : Painter Classic

I take my inspiration from things I'm curious about in every day life. I hope to draw things that stimulate the people who see them through things only I can express.

インスピレーションは日々生活する上で気になっているものから得ています。私にしか出来ない表現で見る人の新しい刺激になる事を願って描いています。

1984年千葉生まれ / 東京在住 / 御茶の水美術専門学校卒

See more artwork(バリエーションはこちら)≫ http://www.pict-web.com/mizuki_abe

013

014

015

016

017

018

Hideo Anze
安瀬 英雄

Media : Tant Paper / Styrene board /
Digital camera / Photoshop CS
画材：タント紙 / スチレンボード /
デジタルカメラ / Photoshop CS

I'm always trying to create expressions of things that people don't do. By making collages of solid models that have been photographed, I aim for a unique interpretation of the world different from computer graphics.

人がやっていないような表現をしたいといつも思って制作しています。撮影した立体の模型をコラージュすることでCGとは違う独特な世界観を目指しました。

1975年東京生まれ / 神奈川在住 / 武蔵野美術大学短期大学部中退

See more artwork（バリエーションはこちら）≫ http://www.pict-web.com/hideo_anze

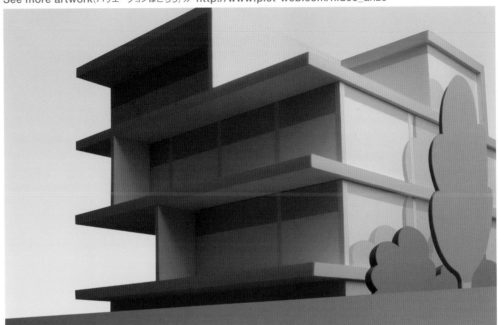

001

002

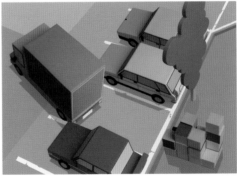

003

004

005

Sachiko Ikoma
生駒 さちこ

Media : Watercolor / Chinese ink / Paper
画材：水彩 / 墨汁 / 紙

I aim to make pictures that brighten up the mood of the people who see them, and to express a lot, with only a few elements. I really like an aspect of casual air, and the atmosphere of people.

少ない要素による豊かな表現、見てくれる人が明るい気持ちになるような絵を目指しています。人のたたずまい、暮らし、なにげない様子が大好きです。

1971年神戸生まれ / 東京在住 / セツ・モードセミナー卒

See more artwork（バリエーションはこちら）≫ http://www.pict-web.com/sachiko_ikoma

001

002

003

004

005

006

Shizuka Ishizaka
石坂 しづか

Media : Photoshop4.0, 6.0 / Color pencil / Pencil
画材 : Photoshop 4.0, 6.0 / 色鉛筆 / 鉛筆

I'm dedicated to creating works that cause the people who see them to smile. I get inspiration from music and journey.

誰かが指さしてクスリと笑ってくれるような作品を作っていきたいとおもいます。インスピレーションを受けるのは音楽と旅。

1971年東京生まれ / 東京在住 / 桑沢デザイン研究所卒

See more artwork(バリエーションはこちら)≫ http://www.pict-web.com/shizuka_ishizaka

020

021

022

023

024

025

あ

Hiroki Itagaki
板垣 広樹

Media : Illustrator CS / Photoshop CS
画材 : Illustrator CS / Photoshop CS

I don't want to forget the feeling of always challenging, new, and interesting things when I'm creating a work.

作品を制作する時は、常に新しいものや面白いものに挑む気持ちを忘れないようにしていきたいと思っています。

1974年埼玉生まれ / 東京在住

See more artwork（バリエーションはこちら）≫ http://www.pict-web.com/hiroki_itagaki

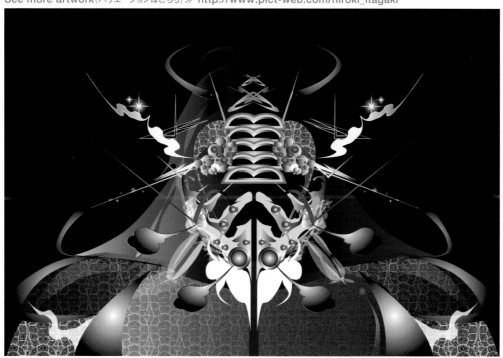

001

002

003

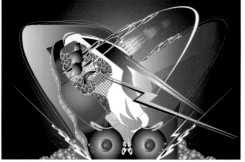

004

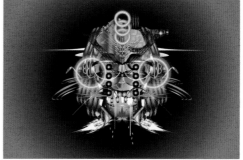

005

Yumi Inaba
いなば ゆみ

Media : Gouache / Photoshop CS
画材：ガッシュ / Photoshop CS

I endeavor to express stylishly and simply, things I ought to convey. A bit of essence is added there, I'm glad if the people who see my work feel happy.

伝えるべき事を、おしゃれにシンプルに表現出来るよう心がけてます。そこに少しのエッセンスを加え、見た人が楽しい気持ちになってもらえたら、嬉しい。

1971年埼玉県生まれ / 目黒区在住 / 山脇美術専門学院卒業

See more artwork（バリエーションはこちら）≫ http://www.pict-web.com/yumi_inaba

022

023

024

025

026

027

Yasufumi Imai
イマイ ヤスフミ

Media : Illustrator CS
画材 : Illustrator CS

While being conscious of the cartoons I saw when I was very young, I construct a world view that feels like "now", through a unique fish-eye view, with both a dynamic speedy feeling, and lots of humor.

『幼い頃見た日本の漫画』を意識しながら独自の魚眼的目線で、ダイナミックかつスピード感、さらににユーモアを盛り込んだ『今』を感じる世界観を構築しています。

1972年大阪府生まれ / 大阪在住 / 大阪芸術大学デザイン学科卒

See more artwork（バリエーションはこちら）≫ http://www.pict-web.com/yasufumi_imai

040

041

042

043

044

Yumi Imai
今井 有美

Media : Powdered Mineral Pigments /
Hide Glue / Chinese Ink / Pencil
画材：水干絵具 / 膠 / 墨汁 / 鉛筆

It all comes down to the fact that I look carefully,
and draw, without crazily taking in an interpretation.

変に解釈を入れるのではなく、ちゃんと見て描くということ
に尽きます。何も描かれていない余白をいかに描くか、とい
うことを考えて制作しています。

1974年愛知生まれ / 神奈川在住 / 名古屋芸術大学日本画専攻卒

See more artwork（バリエーションはこちら）≫ http://www.pict-web.com/yumi_imai

001

002

003

004

005

006

Shinichi Imanaka
今中 信一

Media : Acrylic gouache / Pencil
画材：アクリルガッシュ / リキテックス/鉛筆

By eating well, sleeping well, and exercising well, on a routine basis I keep myself fit. I endeavor to focus on creating works at a good time, when I'm in tiptop condition.

ちゃんと食べて、ちゃんと寝て、ちゃんと運動して、普段から体を整えておいて、一番コンディションの良い時間帯に集中して制作するように心がけています。

1966年兵庫県生まれ / 東京在住 / シカゴ美術館付属美術大学(The School of the Art Institute of Chicago) 卒

See more artwork(バリエーションはこちら)≫ http://www.pict-web.com/shinichi_imanaka

034

035

036

037

038

028

Baron Ueda
上田 バロン

Media : Illustrator CS2
画材 : Illustrator CS2

I aloofly draw each person's vision of the world with the features in their eyes. I specialize in creating multi-layered compositions, using lots of smoky colors, knick knacks, and being meticulous about details.

目に特徴を持つ人物でそれぞれの世界観をクールに描く。スモーキーカラーを多用し、ディテールにこだわった小物使いと奥行きを出す画面構成を得意とする。

1974年京都生まれ / 大阪在住 / 大阪コミュニケーションアート卒

See more artwork(バリエーションはこちら)≫ http://www.pict-web.com/baron_ueda

021

022

023

024

025

026

Fumitake Uchida
内田 文武

Media : Photoshop CS / Acrylic
画材 : Photoshop CS / アクリル

In everyday life and the towns I visit, I draw moments that reflect my heart. Using simple colors and large, quiet compositions, I hope I can draw so you can see the passage of time and eternity within a moment in time.

日々の生活や訪れた町で、肌鏡に写る刹那を描く。シンプルな色使い、大きく静かな構図で束の間の内に見える時の経過や永遠を描ければと思っています。

1981年京都府生まれ / 東京在住 / 京都造形芸術大学美術工芸学科卒

See more artwork（バリエーションはこちら）≫ http://www.pict-web.com/fumitake_uchida

033

034

035

036

037

038

Masashi Uno
宇野 将司

Media : Photoshop 7.0 / Illustrator 10.0
画材 : Photoshop 7.0 / Illustrator 10.0

あ

Create works that have a airiness, I carefully treat the spaces at the margin of the work. I am conscious of expression can come into my works by the movement of people's eyes who see them even though they are simple compositions.

空気感のある作品にするために、作品中の余白の扱いを大切にし、シンプルな構成でも見る人の目線の動きで作品に表情を出せるように意識しています。

1978年岐阜生まれ / 岐阜在住 / 岐阜聖徳学園大学附属高等学校卒

See more artwork(バリエーションはこちら)≫ http://www.pict-web.com/masashi_uno

017

018

019

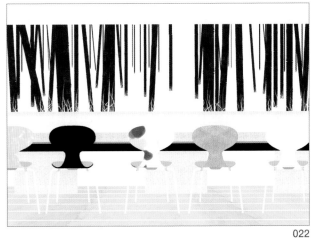

022

020

021

041

Uyo Takayama
うよ 高山

Media : Watercolor / Ink / Pencil / Photoshop
画材：水彩 / インク / 鉛筆 / Photoshop等

I want to draw humor, fun and kindness of people and the world around it with minimal expression. I'm happy if people who view my work can get those feelings.

人やそれをとりまく世界の可笑しさ楽しさ優しさを温度のあるミニマルな表現で描きたい。見てくださった方へ画面から幸せな気分が伝染したら幸せです。

東京都生まれ / 東京在住 / バンタンデザイン研究所卒

See more artwork（バリエーションはこちら）≫ http://www.pict-web.com/takayama_uyo

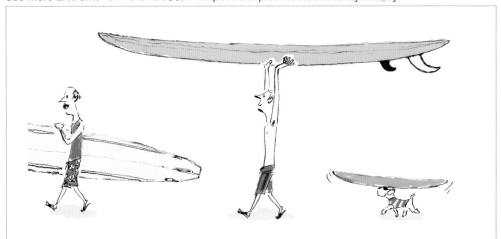

001

002

003

004

005

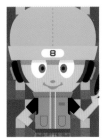

8-bit line
エイトビットライン

I draw digital image by nostalgic feel that is like drawn with dots by 8-bit game machine.

昔の8ビットゲーム機のドットで描いたような、懐かしくもデジタルなイメージを表現しています。

Media : illustrator CS
画材 : illustrator CS

1972年大阪府生まれ / 大阪在住 / 大阪芸術大学デザイン学科卒

See more artwork（バリエーションはこちら）≫ http://www.pict-web.com/8-bit_line

Endoko
エンドコ
（エンドウ図案工場）

Media : Illustrator 9.0
画材 : Illustrator 9.0

I specialize in retro-modern taste. I treasure the feeling of always having my antennas out.

レトロモダンテイストを得意としております。いつもアンテナをはりめぐらして感じることを大切にしています。

1974年静岡生まれ / 神奈川在住 / 武蔵野美術短期大学美術科卒

See more artwork（バリエーションはこちら）≫ http://www.pict-web.com/endoko

001

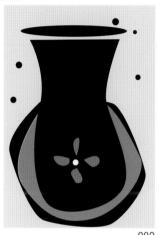

002

003

004

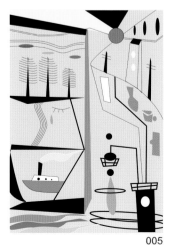

005

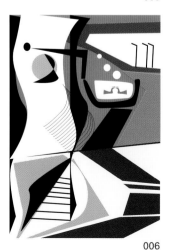

006

Miyuki Ohashi
大橋 美由紀

Media : Acrylic / Crayon / Pencil
画材：アクリル / クレヨン / 鉛筆

I mainly draw chic, stylish women. My objective is to create daring yet elegant illustrations that do not follow fashion too closely.

おしゃれでシックな女性をメインに描いています。流行に流され過ぎない、大胆だけれど品を失わないイラストを目標にしています。

1976年栃木県生まれ / 東京在住 / セツ・モードセミナー卒

See more artwork（バリエーションはこちら）≫ http://www.pict-web.com/miyuki_ohashi

061

062

063

064

065

066

Shinko Okuhara
奥原 しんこ

Media : Acrylic / Photographs / Printed papers
画材：アクリル絵具 / 写真 / 雑誌等印刷物

I've been trying to transpose into colors the sounds, smell, and airiness that I see in the various places I actually walk.

実際に歩いた様々な場所の音や匂いや空気を色に置き換えて表現するようにしている。

1973年宮城県生まれ / 東京在住 /
横浜美術短期大学、セツ・モードセミナー卒業

See more artwork（バリエーションはこちら）≫ http://www.pict-web.com/shinko_okuhara

021

022

023

024

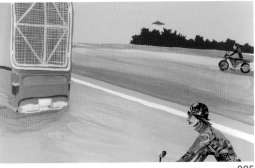

025

Ayako Ochi
おち あやこ

Media : Photoshop 6.0 / Acrylic / Pencil
画材 : Photoshop 6.0 / アクリル / 鉛筆

1967年大阪府生まれ / 東京在住 / Masa Mode Academy of Art 卒

I try to make the kind of compositions that don't offend anyone's sensibilities.

作品を見ていただくすべての方が嫌な気持ちにならないような作品作りを心掛けています。

See more artwork (バリエーションはこちら) ≫ http://www.pict-web.com/ayako_ochi

001
002
003
004
005
006

Licaco Kaquta
かくた りかこ

Media : Photoshop CS2
画材 : Photoshop CS2

I think the most important thing is to enjoy drawing. Whenever I get the feeling "that's cool." I treasure it. I want to change constantly without being constrained by my past self.

楽しんで描くことを一番に考えています。その時「かっこいい」と思う気持ちを大切に。これまでの自分の枠にとらわれず、常に変化していきたいです。

神戸生まれ / 東京在住 / 神戸文化短期大学デザイン美術科卒

か

See more artwork（バリエーションはこちら）≫ http://www.pict-web.com/licaco_kaquta

017

016

018

019

020

021

Sara Kajino
梶野 沙羅

Media : Silkscreen / Photoshop 10.0 / Illustrator 7.0
画材：シルクスクリーン / Photoshop10.0 / Illustrator 7.0

Illustrations are a world of imagination. I want to draw pictures which expand the world of the people who see them, through the images in my pictures.

イラストは想像の世界です。私のイメージから見る人の世界が広がってゆくような絵を描いてゆきたいと考えます。

1982年愛知県生まれ / 東京在住/東京芸術大学美術学部デザイン科卒 同大学デザイン科修士課程在学中

か

See more artwork（バリエーションはこちら）≫ http://www.pict-web.com/sara_kajino

001

002

003

004

005

006

Eri Katayama
片山 エリ

Media : Colorpencil / Pencil / Watercolor / Photoshop6.0
画材：色鉛筆 / 鉛筆 / 水彩 / ペン / Photoshop6.0

I draw from my senses. I get my inspiration from daily life; nature, plants, people's movement, memory, music, etc.

感覚で描くこと。自然、植物、人の動き、記憶、音楽など日常の中からインスピレーションを受けています。

1978年愛知県生まれ / 愛知在住 /
愛知県立芸術大学美術学部デザイン科卒業

か

See more artwork（バリエーションはこちら）≫ http://www.pict-web.com/eri_katayama

001

002

003

004

005

006

Aya Kato
加藤 彩

Media : Photoshop 7.0 / Illustrator 10 /
Watercolor / Chinese Ink
画材 : Photoshop 7.0 / Illustrator 10 / 水彩 / 墨

I would like to draw art works that wake up inactive soul deep in people's mind. And I would like to carry on the Japanese spirit protected by samurai for his life. I describe such ambition in my art work.

人の心の奥に眠っている魂を呼び起こすような作品を描きたい。そして、侍が命懸けで護ってきた日本精神を未来へ繋げたい、そのような想いを作品の上に重ねています。

1982年愛知生まれ / 愛知在住 / 愛知教育大学美術科卒

See more artwork(バリエーションはこちら)≫ http://www.pict-web.com/aya_kato

001

002

003

004

005

Mari Katogi
加藤木 麻莉

Media : Acrylic
画材：アクリル

I want to draw illustrations that are conscious of fashion and gracious tones.

ファッション性と上品な色調を意識したイラストを描いて行きたいです。

1981年茨城県生まれ / 東京在住 / セツ・モードセミナー卒

か

See more artwork(バリエーションはこちら) ≫ http://www.pict-web.com/mari_katogi

001

002

003

004

005

006

Hiroshi Kato
加藤 大

Media : Postercolor / Wartercolor / Oil pastel /
Cloth
画材：ポスターカラー / 水彩 / オイルパステル /
布

Not becoming too sweet.

甘くなりすぎないこと。

1972年愛知県生まれ / 東京在住 / 日大芸術学部美術学科卒

See more artwork（バリエーションはこちら）≫ http://www.pict-web.com/hiroshi_kato

001

002

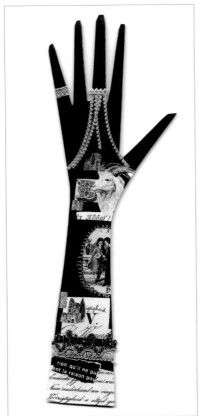

003

004

005

006

En hiver...

J'aime la neige

Fuko Kawamura
河村 ふうこ

Media : Photoshop CS2
画材 : Photoshop CS2

I'm dedicated to drawing with a warm and happy feeling. Within a casual life you can receive inspiration, however, I want to draw pictures that are simple, and in which people can see stories.

暖かく、幸せな気持ちで描くように、心がけています。何気ない生活の中でインスピレーションを受けますが、シンプルでいて、物語を感じる絵を描いていきたい。

1968年東京都生まれ / 東京在住 / 清泉女子大学英文科

か

See more artwork(バリエーションはこちら) ≫ http://www.pict-web.com/fuko_kawamura

032

033

034

035

036

037

Mitsunari Kawamoto
川本 光成

Media : Chinese ink / Watercolor / Pencil /
Pen / Gold leaf / Photoshop 6.0 / Illustrator 9.0
画材：墨 / 水溶性絵具 / 鉛筆 / ペン / 金箔 /
Photoshop 6.0 / Illustrator 9.0

I get inspiration from all things, regardless of
whether they are ordinary or extraordinary. I make
them into my own form as much as possible.

日常、非日常問わず、ほとんどすべてのものからインスピレ
ーションを受けてしまいます。そこから湧き上がって押さえら
れないものを、ひとつでも多く自分の形にしていくのです。

1971年愛知県生まれ / 名古屋在住 /
名古屋造形芸術大学デザイン学科卒

か

See more artwork〈バリエーションはこちら〉≫ http://www.pict-web.com/mitsunari_kawamoto

001

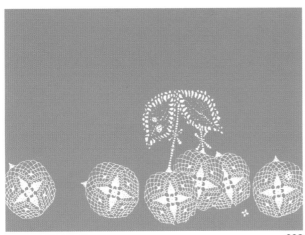

002

003

004

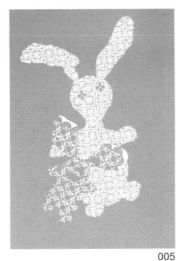

005

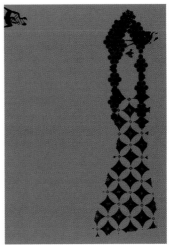

006

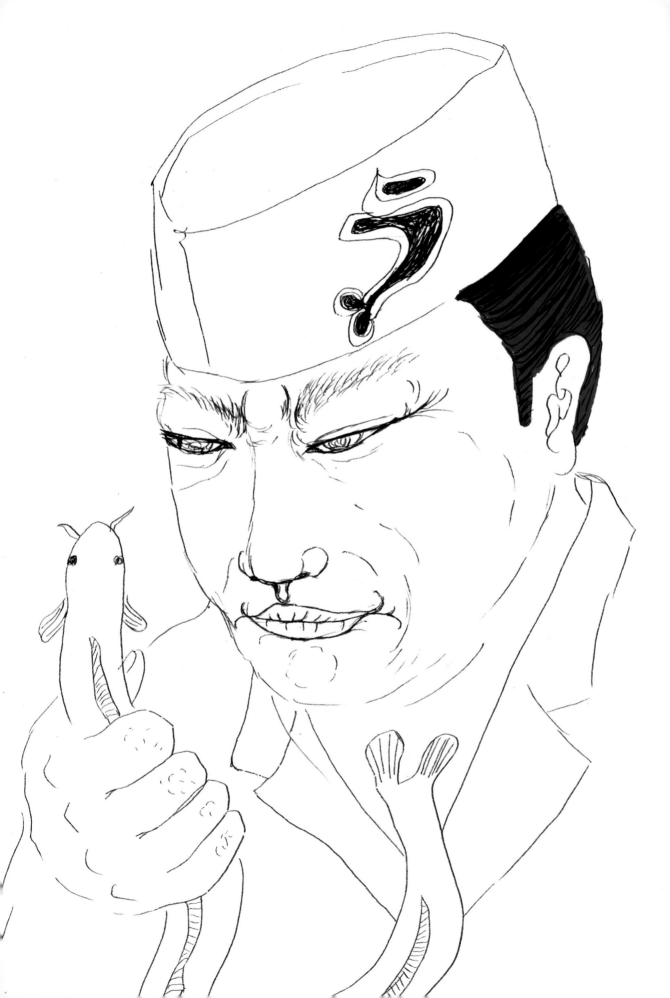

Sen Kanno
菅野 旋

Media : Ballpoint Pen / Marker
画材：ボールペン / マジックペン

First, the spirit of line. Second the thickness of the line, Third, a bit of humorous feeling. Fourth, a bit of melancholy. Fifth not putting so much down on the page when I draw.

その1、線の勢い。その2、線の太さ。その3、ちょっと笑える感じ。その4、ちょっとのメランコリック。その5、あまり描き込まないようにすること。

1969年生まれ / 東京在住 / バンタンデザイン研究所卒

See more artwork（バリエーションはこちら）≫ http://www.pict-web.com/sen_kanno

008

009

010

011

012

013

Hiromi Kishi
岸 弘海

Media : Chinese ink / Banboo pencil / Pen
画材：墨汁 / 竹ペン / つけペン

Feel the power of the object, the power of penetrating the object, and the power of the image. I think I have been successful if the people who look at my work can imagine something.

ものを感じるちから、ものを読み解く力と想像力。私の絵を見た人が、何か空想して下さったなら、成功だと思ってます。

1973年生まれ / 大阪在住

See more artwork（バリエーションはこちら）≫ http://www.pict-web.com/hiromi_kishi

099

100

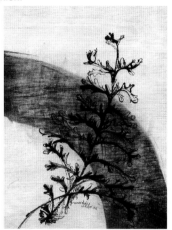

101

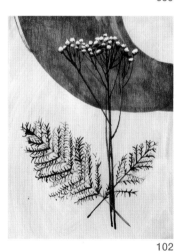

102

103

104

105

106

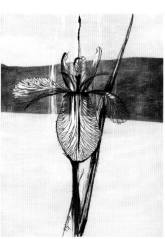

107

Heisuke Kitazawa
北沢 平祐：PCP

Media : Digital / Acrylic
画材：デジタル / アクリル

When I create my work, I try not to force my philosophy and values to my viewers, and try to create work with diverse perspective and meanings, so each and every viewer can create their own story within my work.

絵によってひとつの思想や価値観を押し付けるのではなく、見てくれた方の想像力をかきたて、それぞれのユニークな答えが出るような絵を描きたいと思っています。また、独りよがりにならない程度に自分も楽しめる作品を作りたいです。

1976年神奈川生まれ／神奈川在住／カリフォルニア州立大学フラートン校、大学院卒

か

See more artwork（バリエーションはこちら）≫ http://www.pict-web.com/heisuke_kitazawa

001

002

003

004

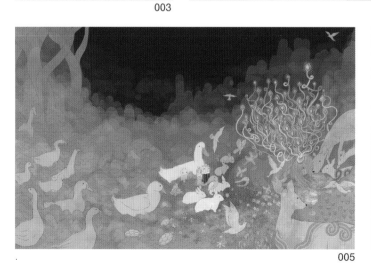

005

006

Shin Kikkawa
桔川 伸

Media : Acrylic
画材：アクリル

Processing and reconstructing images. Interspace, surreal, and collage and rock.

イメージの咀嚼、および再構築。空気感、シュール、コラージュ、ロック。

1974年東京都生まれ /
東京在住/千代田工科芸術専門学校イラストレーション科卒

See more artwork(バリエーションはこちら)≫ http://www.pict-web.com/shin_kikkawa

001

002

003

004

005

006

Toshiko Kimura
木村 敏子

Media : Ballpoint Pen / Photoshop CS
画材：ボールペン / Photoshop CS

Although it is too subtle to care about, I pursue with persistence the feeling and air of memory inside me without passing over, nor looking away, I also treasure humor.

自分の中の微妙すぎてどうでもいい感情や記憶の空気を、見逃さず、目をそらさず、しつこく追求すること。あとユーモアを大事にしています。

1978年埼玉県生まれ / 東京在住 /
創形美術学校ビジュアルデザイン科卒業

See more artwork（バリエーションはこちら）≫ http://www.pict-web.com/toshiko_kimura

001

002

003

004

005

Nobuo Kusunoki
楠 伸生

Media : Photoshop 5.02
画材 : Photoshop 5.02

I don't just want to draw human figures, but also still-lives and scenerywith a world that I can express as much as possible by simplistic touch, andI cherish colors and forms that feel space as a blank.

余白としての空間を感じる色やフォルムを大切にして、なるべく簡略化したタッチで表現できる世界を、人物だけでなく、静物や風景なども描いていきたいです。

1958年大阪府生まれ / 東京都在住

See more artwork（バリエーションはこちら）》 http://www.pict-web.com/nobuo_kusunoki

065

066

067

068

069

070

Yukiko Kusunoki
楠 裕紀子

Media : Photoshop 5.02
画材 : Photoshop 5.02

I take pride in the lifestyle of women living today with a lot of vitality, who don't forget a playful heart. So give me a call if you want to express stylish women!

元気旺盛で遊び心も忘れない、今を生きる女性達のライフスタイルを得意としています。スタイリッシュな女性達の表現ならぜひどうぞ!

1959年兵庫県生まれ / 東京在住 / 武庫川女子短期大学服飾科卒

See more artwork(バリエーションはこちら) ≫ http://www.pict-web.com/yukiko_kusunoki

032

033

034

035

036

037

Reiko Kusumoto
楠本 礼子

Media : Photoshop 5.5
画材 : Photoshop 5.5

The airiness over there. Various people are there, various feelings are there. I hope to create expressions that evoke even subtle heart patterns.

そこにある空気感。いろいろな人間がいて、いろいろな気持ちがあって。微妙なこころ模様さえ感じ取れるような表現が出来たらと思う。

熊本県生まれ / 神奈川在住 /
武蔵野美術大学 空間演出デザイン学科卒

か

See more artwork(バリエーションはこちら)≫ http://www.pict-web.com/reiko_kusumoto

009

010

011

012

013

014

Yuki Koinuma
コイヌマユキ

Media : Crayon / Color pencil / Pencil / Pen /
Photoshop CS2
画材：クレヨン / 色鉛筆 / 鉛筆 / ペン /
Photoshop CS2

I hope to express straightforwardly a feeling of being in the air. Beauty, sadness, loveliness, happiness, I hope to be able to draw these things.

空気の中で感じることを、素直に表現できたらと思っています。きれい、かなしい、愛しい、嬉しい、そういうものを絵にできたらと思います。

1980年神奈川生まれ / 埼玉在住 /
多摩美術大学グラフィックデザイン学科卒

か

See more artwork（バリエーションはこちら）≫ http://www.pict-web.com/yuki_koinuma

001

002

003

004

005

006

Ayako Kozen
コウゼン アヤコ

Media : Acrylic gouache
画材：アクリルガッシュ

I aim to draw images that feel like easygoing time and air that are based on things that I see in daily life and things that move me.

日常生活で目にしたこと、感じたことなどをもとに、ゆったりした時間や空気を感じられる画面作りを目指して描いています。

1974年京都生まれ / 京都在住 / 京都市立芸術大学美術科卒

See more artwork（バリエーションはこちら）≫ http://www.pict-web.com/ayako_kozen

068

069

070

071

072

073

KO-ZOU
KO-ZOU

Media : Illustrator 10 / Photoshop 7
画材 : Illustrator 10 / Photoshop 7

I take care of the first vague image that come out from the influence of the scenes that I usually see around my neighborhood, television, magazines, and music.

普段よく見ている近所の景色、テレビ、雑誌、音楽等から影響を受けて出て来た、最初の漠然としたイメージを大事にしてます。

1981年愛媛県生まれ / 東京在住 / 中京大学メディア学科卒

See more artwork〈バリエーションはこちら〉≫ http://www.pict-web.com/ko_zou

026

027

028

029

030

Natsuko Kozue
梢 夏子

Media : Japanese style Painting colors /
Powdered mineral pigments / colorpencil /
Acrylic
画材：日本画用顔料 / 岩絵具 / 色鉛筆 /
アクリル等

I always draw like I spell; images that always come
from words. Also, using drawing materials that are
particular to Japanese paintings, I produce a specific texture.

いつも言葉から創造して行くイメージを綴るように描いてい
ます。また、日本画独自の画材を使い独特な質感を醸し出
しています。

1980年大分県生まれ / 京都在住 / 成安造形短期大学美術専攻科卒

See more artwork(バリエーションはこちら) ≫ http://www.pict-web.com/natsuko_kozue

001

002

003

004

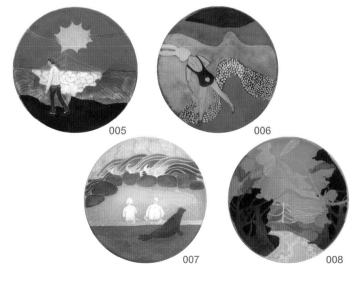

005

006

007

008

Aki Kobayashi
小林 晃

Media : Acrylic gouache / Photoshop 5.5
画材：アクリルガッシュ / Photoshop 5.5

Sometimes I imagine air, light, etc. in scenes from old books and movies. I want to draw a world that exists in places that I don't have personal experience with.

古い映画や本などから　その情景にある空気や光などを想像したりすることがあります。そんな自分の知らないどこかで存在している世界を描きたいです。

1978年栃木県生まれ / 東京在住 / セツ・モードセミナー卒

See more artwork（バリエーションはこちら）≫ http://www.pict-web.com/aki_kobayashi

027

028

029

030

031

032

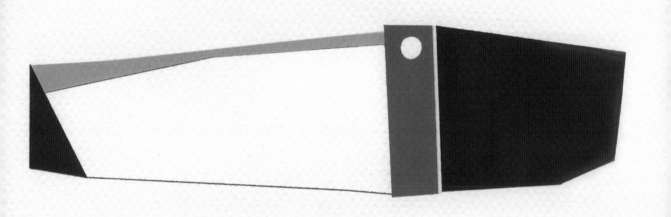

Ayumi Kobayashi
小林 愛美

Media : Acrylic / Gouache / Pen / Pencil /
Ruler / Masking tape
画材：アクリル / ガッシュ / ペン / 鉛筆 / 定規 /
マスキングテープ

I austerely create things with motifs of scenes and things close to me, using rulers and masking tape. I want to express a down to earth nostalgia and modernity.

身近にあるモノや風景をモチーフに、定規とマスキングテープを使ってシンプルに制作。素朴になつかしさとモダンさを表現したいと思っています。

1964年愛媛生まれ / 千葉在住 / セツ・モードセミナー卒

か

See more artwork（バリエーションはこちら）≫ http://www.pict-web.com/ayumi_kobayashi

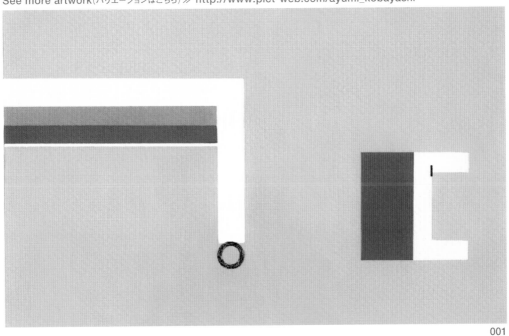

001

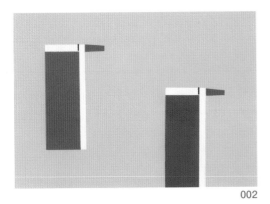

002

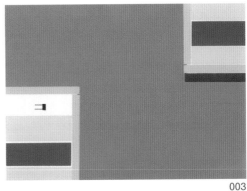

003

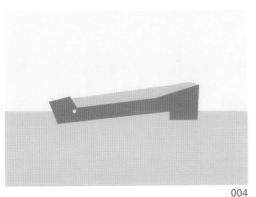

004

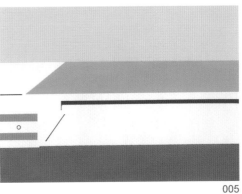

005

Misao Kobayashi
こばやし みさを

Media : Acrylic / Colorpencil
画材：アクリル / 色鉛筆

I have in mind simple expression with few colors. I'm always looking for combinations of beautiful colors from scenery in nature and from within the city.

色数の少ないシンプルな表現を心がけています。キレイな色の組合せを自然や街の中の風景からいつも探しています。

1974年山口県生まれ / 大阪在住 / 立命館大学産業社会学科卒

か

See more artwork（バリエーションはこちら）≫ http://www.pict-web.com/misao_kobayashi

023

024

025

026

027

028

Yusuke Saitoh
サイトウ ユウスケ

Media : Photoshop CS / Painter 8
画材 : Photoshop CS / Painter 8

Positive things. I communicate through my works.

ポジティブであること。作品を通じてのコミュニケーション。

1978年神奈川県生まれ / 東京都在住 /
バンタンデザイン研究所イラストレーション科卒

See more artwork（バリエーションはこちら）≫ http://www.pict-web.com/yusuke_ saitoh

010

012

013

014

Shigeyuki Sakata
さかた しげゆき

Media : Photoshop 6.0 / Illustrator 8.0
画材 : Photoshop 6.0 / Illustrator 8.0

I create works in which even in happiness, nostalgia and anguish can be felt. I keep occurrences in everyday life in mind and make use of them in my works.

楽しさのなかにも懐かしさ、切なさを感じられる作品を作っています。普段の生活の中での出来事を心に留めておき、作品に生かしています。

1973年神奈川県生まれ / 東京在住 / 京都造形芸術大学デザイン科卒

See more artwork（バリエーションはこちら）≫ http://www.pict-web.com/shigeyuki_sakata

さ

015

016

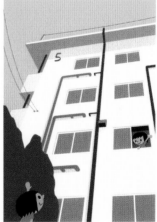

017

018

019

020

103

Nao Sakamoto
坂本 奈緒

Media : Ballpoint Pen / Photoshop CS
画材 : ボールペン / 筆ペン / Photoshop CS

I hope to make the kind of pictures that give a sense of the air.

空気が伝わるような絵がかければ、と思っております。

1979年北海道生まれ / 神奈川県在住 /
コム・イラストレーターズ・スタジオ修了

さ

See more artwork (バリエーションはこちら) ≫ http://www.pict-web.com/nao_sakamoto

001

002

003

004

005

006

sakilica
さきりか

Media : Photoshop CS2
画材 : Photoshop CS2

Become audacious and a lots of attention to detail.

大胆になること、そして細部までこだわること。

神戸生まれ / 東京在住 / 神戸文化短期大学デザイン美術科卒

See more artwork(バリエーションはこちら)≫ http://www.pict-web.com/sakilica

001

002

003

004

005

006

Noriko Sakurai
櫻井 乃梨子

Media : Watercolor / Acrylic / Pencil / Colorpencil
画材：水彩 / アクリル / 鉛筆 / 色鉛筆

Being healthy, having fun, and always doing my best. With regards to my pictures, I am careful to create space and nuances without logic.

健康であること、楽しむこと、常に一生懸命であることと絵に関しては理屈でないニュアンスや「間」を大切に創作しています。

1971年広島生まれ / 東京在住 / セツ・モードセミナー卒

さ

See more artwork（バリエーションはこちら）≫ http://www.pict-web.com/noriko_sakurai

001

002

003

004

005

006

Shunsuke Satake
サタケ シュンスケ

Media : Photoshop CS / Illustrator CS
画材 : Photoshop CS / Illustrator CS

I create as I think about how I can see people and objects roughly, and represent them clearly. I don't flatter too much, but people who see my work somehow love it. I pursue that kind of sweetness.

人や物をいかに大きく捉え、明解に伝えるかを考え創作しています。媚びすぎず、でもどこか愛しやすい。そんな可愛らしさを追求しています。

1981年大阪府生まれ / 大阪在住 /
神戸デザイナー学院グラフィックデザイン学科卒

See more artwork（バリエーションはこちら）≫ http://www.pict-web.com/shunsuke_satake

さ

013

014

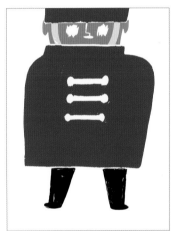

015

016

017

018

111

Kazunori Sadahiro
サダヒロ カズノリ

Media : Photoshop 7.0 / Illustrator 10 /
Color pen / Sticker / Maskingtape
画材 : Photoshop 7.0 / Illustrator 10 /
カラーペン / シール / マスキングテープ

I draw a wide range of objects, from abstraction to
the concrete. I take care in creating warmth and
refined shapes.

抽象から具象まで幅広く描いています。洗練された形と、手
作りの温かさを大切にしています。

1969年山口県生まれ / 東京在住 /
武蔵野美術大学短期大学部デザイン科卒

さ

See more artwork（バリエーションはこちら）≫ http://www.pict-web.com/kazunori_sadahiro

001

002

003

004

005

006

Ayumi Sato
さとう あゆみ

Media : Photoshop 7.0
画材 : Photoshop 7.0

I'm dedicated to illustrations in which people can see elegance somewhere. I hope to continue to draw translucent women from now on.

どこかに品を感じるイラストを心がけています。透明感のある女性をこれからも描き続けていきたいと思っています。

長野県生まれ / 東京在住 / 東京家政大学短期大学部服飾美術科卒

さ

See more artwork (バリエーションはこちら)≫ http://www.pict-web.com/ayumi_sato

013

014

015

016

017

018

115

Shigemi Sato
佐藤 繁

Maximize the effect of hand drawing considering color combination and airiness. I'm dedicated to deliver the atmosphere and airiness which I wish to communicate.

色合いや空気感を大切に手描きのタッチをいかして描いています。伝えたい雰囲気や空気が届くようにと心がけています。

Media : Watercolor / Acrylic
画材：水彩 / アクリル

東京生まれ / 東京在住 / セツ・モードセミナー卒

See more artwork（バリエーションはこちら）》 http://www.pict-web.com/shigemi_sato

さ

001

002

003

004

005

Ryuji Shishido
宍戸 竜二

I'm trying to take in the things on the inner side of myself, not being distracted by what's around me. I believe that drawing whatever that is becomes the individuality that is myself.

周りに気を取られず自分の内側にある物を取り入れるようにしています。それがどんなものを描こうと自分自身という個性になると信じています。

Media : Illustrator 8.0, CS2 / PhotoShop CS2 / Gauze
画材 : Illustrator 8.0, CS2 / PhotoShop CS2 / ガーゼ

1972年神奈川生まれ / 神奈川在住

さ

See more artwork〈バリエーションはこちら〉≫ http://www.pict-web.com/ryuji_shishido

001

002

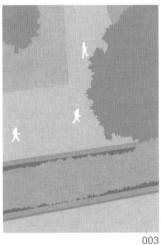

003

004

005

006

007

119

Yu Shichiji
七字 由布

Media : Oil Crayon / Color Pencil /
Acrylic gouache
画材：オイルクレパス / 色鉛筆 / アクリルガッシュ

When I find beautiful colors and lines in life, I draw something because I want to leave it in the drawing to show someone else.

生活の中で綺麗な色や線を見つけたら、他の誰かにも伝えたくてそれを絵に残したいと思って描きます。

1983年埼玉生まれ / 埼玉在住 / イラストレーション青山塾修了

See more artwork（バリエーションはこちら）≫ http://www.pict-web.com/yu_shichiji

001

002

003

004

005

Keiko Shibata
柴田 ケイコ

Media : Oil Pastel / Color pencil / Fabric / Paper/
画材：オイルパステル / 色鉛筆 / クラフト紙 / 布 / 紙

I cherish continually making images of the colors, scenes, living things, air, etc. in my everyday life that I feel with my whole body as soon as I meet them.

日常生活の中で出会った瞬間に感じた色、景色、生き物、空気感など自分自身全体で受けとめ、それをイメージし続ける事を大切にしています。

1973年高知生まれ /
高知在住/奈良芸術短期大学ヴィジュアルデザイン学科卒

See more artwork（バリエーションはこちら）≫ http://www.pict-web.com/keiko_shibata

001

002

003

004

005

006

Noritomo Shimizu
志水 則友

Media : Color paper / Color pencil / Glue
画材：色画用紙 / 色鉛筆 / のり

I started my technique because I thought it was interesting to design by making collages out of colored Japanese paper. That's a part of my playful heart that I found in my challenges finding how far I can play using colored paper.

ちぎり絵でデッサンをやったらオモシロそうだなと思い、始めた技法です。色紙を使ってどこまで遊べるか、という自分への課題の中で見つけた遊び心の一端です。

1974年千葉県生まれ / 東京在住 / 東洋美術専門学校卒

See more artwork（バリエーションはこちら）≫ http://www.pict-web.com/noritomo_shimizu

さ

014

015

016

017

018

019

Yoichi Shimoda
下田 洋一

Media : Watercolor
画材：水彩絵具

I hope to deeply ponder for a long time what I shouldn't draw, as much as, or more than, what I should draw.

何を描くかということ同様、あるいはそれ以上に、何を描かないかということを常日頃から深く思索していきたいと思います。

1972年東京生まれ / 東京在住 / セツ・モードセミナー卒

See more artwork（バリエーションはこちら）≫ http://www.pict-web.com/yoichi_shimoda

さ

029

030

031

032

033

034

Fumiko Shukuya
宿谷 フミコ

Media : Acrylic / Marker / Ink / Pencil
画材 : アクリル / マーカー / インク / 鉛筆

I'm dedicated to bringing out the good feeling, colors, and spaces. On a daily basis, I come up against something with fairly vivid colors, and images of creation come to mind.

気持ちの良い色と間がだせるように心がけています。日々何かちょっとした鮮やかな色に出会うと創作のイメージが浮かびます。

1970年生まれ / 東京在住 / セツ・モードセミナー卒

See more artwork (バリエーションはこちら) ≫ http://www.pict-web.com/fumiko_shukuya

001

002

003

004

005

006

Jun Watanabe
Jun Watanabe

Media : Illustrator 10 / Photoshop CS / FASKOLOR
画材 : Illustrator 10 / Photoshop CS / FASKOLOR

Creating an environment where I can spend a lot of time to do what I like, and leading a life in which I can do that naturally. The inscription by my side is "Jun Watanabe's Hobby Japan".

好きなことにたくさん時間を費やせる環境作りと、それが自然にできる生活を送ること。座右の銘は「JunWatanabe流のホビージャパン」。

1977年新潟県生まれ / 千葉在住 / 東京デザイナー学院卒

See more artwork（バリエーションはこちら）≫ http://www.pict-web.com/jun_watanabe

さ

001

002

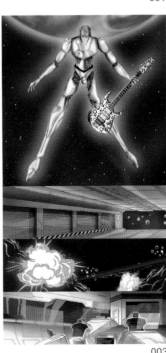

003

Yohei Sugiyama
杉山 陽平

Media : Photoshop CS / Illustrator CS / Dyes / Acrylic
画材 : Photoshop CS / Illustrator CS / 染料 / アクリル

I create works by both computer and by hand, aiming to make illustrations that look like they were designed by an illustrator, through illustrations drawn by a designer. And I take care of the Japanese heart when I draw.

デザイナーが描いたイラストで、イラストレーターがデザインしたようなイラストを目標に、手描きとパソコンの両方で制作しています。そして和の心を大切に絵を描いています。JAGDA会員。

1980年金沢生まれ / 金沢美術工芸大学視覚デザイン科卒

See more artwork（バリエーションはこちら）》 http://www.pict-web.com/yohei_sugiyama

さ

001

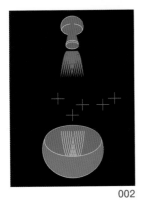

002

003

004

005

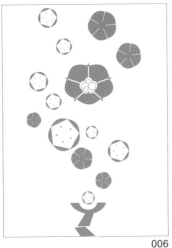

006

007

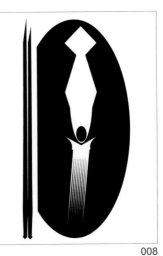

008

Asako Suzuki
すずき あさこ

Media : Illustrator 8.0
画材 : Illustrator 8.0

1977年千葉県生まれ / 東京在住 /
武蔵野美術大学空間演出デザイン科卒

I'm dedicated to creating works that seem to have a bit of a bitter flavor, even in joy and familiarity.

楽しさと親しみやすさの中に、ちょっぴりビターな味わいも感じられるような作品作りを心がけています。

See more artwork（バリエーションはこちら）≫ http://www.pict-web.com/asako_suzuki

001

002

003

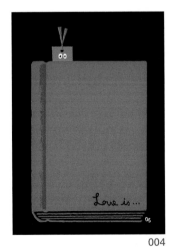

004

005

006

007

Sayaka Suwa
諏訪 さやか

Media : Pencil / Watercolor / Colored ink
画材：鉛筆 / 水彩絵の具 / カラーインク

I draw woman who have both sides; that extraordinary face in fashion magazines or on the stage, and a simple and ordinary face in town or at home.

ファッション雑誌や舞台の上の非日常と、街や家の中でのごくありふれた日常のどちらをも含んだ女性を描くということ。

1980年鹿児島生まれ / 東京在住 / 鹿児島大学法文学部人文学科卒

See more artwork（バリエーションはこちら）》 http://www.pict-web.com/sayaka_suwa

さ

001

002

003

004

005

006

Natsko Seki
せき なつこ

Media : Photoshop CS / Pencil /
Antique Book / Antique Magazine
画材 : Aphotoshop CS / 鉛筆 / 古本 / 古雑誌

I make collages out of interesting prints I have found from the 1950s and 60s. My aim is to create upbeat and humorous works. I'm currently working in London.

50、60年代の古い印刷物の中から、気になるイメージを見つけてはコラージュ。陽気でユーモラスな作品を目指してロンドンにて活動中。

1976年高知生まれ / ロンドン在住 /
ブライトン大学イラストレーション科卒

See more artwork（バリエーションはこちら）≫ http://www.pict-web.com/natsko_seki

011

012

013

014

015

016

"PICT doesn't represent Natsko Seki outside of Japan"

Mihoko Seki
関 美穂子

Media : paints
画材：顔料

I create with a "Katazome" techinique (a traditional Japanese form of tie-dying). While I'm thinking to try to create in some way an unusual air,and I have a premonition that something might happen, I dye.

型染めという技法で制作しています。何かが起きるかも知れない予感の時のどこか非日常な空気を醸し出せたら…と思いながら染めています。

1980年生まれ / 神奈川県横浜市出身 / 京都在住 /
別府大学短期大学部（初等教育科）卒

さ

See more artwork（バリエーションはこちら）≫ http://www.pict-web.com/mihoko_seki

001

002

003

004

005

006

Lena Sonoda
園田 レナ

Media : Ink / Acrylic / Watercolor
画材：インク / 水彩 / アクリル

Aim to impart to the people who view my works, the vitality and euphoria in the figures I draw, by carefully making a world of compositions that live in between everyday life and fantasy.

日常とファンタジーの間に生きるような作品世界を大切に、描く人物がいきいきと幸福感があるように、それを見てくれる人々に伝わるように心掛けています。

1973年神奈川生まれ / 東京在住 / セツ・モードセミナー卒

さ

See more artwork（バリエーションはこちら）≫ http://www.pict-web.com/lena_sonoda

019

020

021

022

023

024

Takashi Taima
泰間 敬視

Media : Plywood / Varnish / Gesso
画材 : シナベニヤ / 水性ニス / ジェッソ

Funny, enjoyable, happy, cute, beautiful, interesting, cool. It's great if I can shut away even one of those feeling in my drawings.

可笑しい、楽しい、嬉しい、可愛い、美しい、面白い、格好良い。そんな感じの一部でも、絵の中に閉じこめることが出来たらなあ。

1971年大阪府生まれ / 東京在住

See more artwork（バリエーションはこちら）≫ http://www.pict-web.com/takashi_taima

013

014

015

016

017

018

145

Hiroko Takashino
高篠 裕子

Media : Watercolor / Gouache / Pencil
画材：水彩 / ガッシュ / 鉛筆

I want to express comfortable space that imparts everyday warmth, enjoyment, and beauty with my original point of view. I hope to make compositions that cause the people who see them to smile.

日常の温かさ、楽しさ、美しさが伝わる心地良い空間を独自の視点で表現したい。見てくれた方に微笑んでもらえるような作品作りを心がけている。

1983年 東京都生まれ / 東京在住 /
文化服装学院アパレルデザイン科卒業

See more artwork(バリエーションはこちら) ≫ http://www.pict-web.com/hiroko_takashino

024

025

026

001

003

011

た

Nobumasa Takahashi
高橋 信雅

I'm a "matiére" maniac who uses the style of combining images that is called mixed media. I study about matiére and present it at a one-person show, which I put my own concept into the lines.

ミクストメディアという混合画法を用いるマチエルマニア。マチエルを研究して年に一度、独自のコンセプトを線にのせた個展にて発表中。

Media : Mixed media
画材：ミクストメディア（混合画法）

1973年神奈川生まれ / 東京在住 /
桑沢デザイン研究所リビングデザイン科卒

See more artwork（バリエーションはこちら）≫ http://www.pict-web.com/nobumasa_takahashi

001

002

003

004

005

006

Chiaki Tagami
田上 千晶

Media : Acrylic gouache / Acrylic
画材：アクリルガッシュ / アクリル

Regardless of whether something is familiar or if it comes from the landscape of a far away country, I endeavor to draw so that people that see my work can feel the air and the presence of motifs.

身近なものでも遠い国の風景でも、モチーフの空気感、気配を感じられるように心掛けて描いています。

東京在住 / セツ・モードセミナー卒

See more artwork（バリエーションはこちら）》 http://www.pict-web.com/chiaki_tagami

008

009

010

011

012

013

Yoshi Tajima
田嶋 吉信

Media : Pencil / Pen / Ink / Acryl /
Photoshop 5.5 / Illustrator 8.0
画材：鉛筆 / ペン / インク / アクリル /
Photoshop 5.5 / Illustrator 8.0

Fantasy and romance. When I create, I don't try to
control everything myself, I enjoy participating in
objective creativity like "l'ecriture automatique"
and love happy mistakes and accidents.

ファンタジーとロマンス。創作時はすべてを自分でコントロ
ールしようとせず、「客観的に創造に参加する」ことを楽しん
でいます。

1969年千葉県生まれ／東京都在住 / American Intercontinental
University in London, Commercial Art専攻 BA卒業

See more artwork（バリエーションはこちら）≫ http://www.pict-web.com/yoshi_tajima

001

002

003

004

005

006

Michiko Tachimoto
立本 倫子

Media : Acrylic / Pencil / Crayon / Pastel /
Mixed media
画材：アクリル / 鉛筆 / クレヨン /
パステル等混合画材

The experience that I spent in rich natural environment when I was little gives a big influence on my
creativity and its theme. Many of my drawings are
from extended imagination of my childhood memory.

幼少期に過ごした豊かな環境での体験が、現在の作品や
そのテーマに関しても大きくつながっています。幼い頃の記
憶から想像を膨らませ描く事が多いです。

1976年金沢生まれ / 東京在住 / 大阪芸術大学デザイン学科卒

See more artwork（バリエーションはこちら）≫ http://www.pict-web.com/michiko_tachimoto

007

008

009

010

Mariko Tanaka
田中 麻里子

Media : Pencil / Alcohol Marker
画材：鉛筆 / アルコールマーカー

I take care to express cuteness and unique stories. I often get inspiration from music, and the people I meet.

かわいらしさと、独特なストーリーを表現することを大切にしてます。音楽や人との出会いからインスピレーションを受けることが多いです。

1979年宮城生まれ / 東京在住 / 大東文化大学文学部教育学科卒

See more artwork（バリエーションはこちら）≫ http://www.pict-web.com/mariko_tanaka

001

002

003

004

005

006

た

chinatsu
chinatsu

I'm dedicated to creating works which are simple but also make the heart of the people who see them ache. I dream them up through spontaneous lines and glossy patterns.

伸びやかな線と艶やか模様で作り出す、シンプルでありながらせつなさを感じさせる作品作りを心がけています。

Media : Pencil / Watercolor / photoshop CS
画材 : 鉛筆 / 水彩 / photoshop CS

See more artwork（バリエーションはこちら）≫ http://www.pict-web.com/chinatsu

024

025

026

027

028

029

D

THANK

Fish

25g NET. APPROX. 22 LOZENGES

ORIGINAL LOZENGES

ORIGINAL LOZEN...

INGREDIENTS:
SUGAR, LIQUORICE, EDIBLE STARCH,
EDIBLE GUM, MENTHOL, EUCALYPTUS OIL,
...SICUM TINCTURE

Contains only natural ingredients.
No preservatives added.

Original Lozenges
Distributed by: G&A Corporation (S) Pte Ltd.,
No. 15, Scots Road #04 - 01/03,
Thong Teck Building, Singapore 228218.
MANUFACTURED BY: LOFTHOUSE OF FLEETWOOD LTD.,
FLEETWOOD, LANCS, ENGLAND.
www.fishermansfriend.com

LOT 06010155

TRON

2/4

@CHARM

part.com   MADE IN U... Stanford, K   THROW

Charm
チャーム

Media : Colored ink / Scrap paper
画材：カラーインク / 廃材紙

Handwriting and hand made things is my creed.
Because collages become uninteresting when I put
them together systematically, I'm dedicated to not
thinking about things too much.

手描き、手作りが信条です。コラージュはきれいにまとまる
とおもしろく無くなってしまうので、あまり考え過ぎないこと
をこころがけています。

1974年沖縄県生まれ / 東京在住

See more artwork（バリエーションはこちら）≫ http://www.pict-web.com/charm

001

002

003

004

005

006

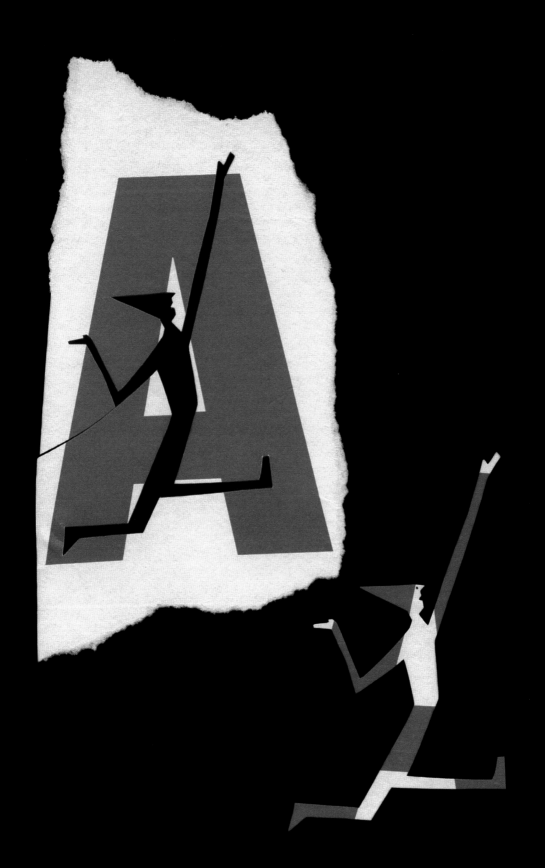

Keiko Tsuji
辻 恵子

Media : Scissors / Pen / Glue /
Papers (Printed Papers etc.)
画材：はさみ / ペン / のり / 紙（印刷物など）

I cut out figures of people using the original colors and patterns on printed materials such as newspapers. There are many hidden shapes not noticeable to us in our daily lives, but I hope through my works, you could see and enjoy them with me.

新聞などに元々ある色を活かして人物像を切り抜いています。日常で何気なく接するものの中にも楽しい形が隠れている事をお見せできれば幸いです。

1975年東京都生まれ / 東京在住 / 文化学院文学科卒

See more artwork（バリエーションはこちら）≫ http://www.pict-web.com/keiko_tsuji

001

002

003

004

005

006

Tomoko Tsuneda
常田 朝子

Media : Pencil / Colored Ink
画材：鉛筆 / カラーインク

Twinkling Twinkling Twinkling, You can see, you can't see. You can hear, you can't hear. You can smell, you can't smell; a pencil in my hand.

キラキラきらきらキラキラきらきら光ってる　見えたり見えなかったり　聞こえたり聞こえなかったり　匂ったり匂わなかったり　手には鉛筆。

1970年東京生まれ / 東京在住 /
武蔵野美術大学短期大学部グラフィックデザイン科卒

See more artwork（バリエーションはこちら）≫ http://www.pict-web.com/tomoko_tsuneda

022

023

024

025

weather forecast

Akemi Tezuka
てづか あけみ

Media : Photoshop 5.5 / CS
画材 : Photoshop 5.5 / CS

The things are accepted by anyone, regardless of their generation or whether they are a man or a woman." I draw, taking care of the point of view, that illustrations exist mixed up in life.

「年代性別問わず受け入れられるもの」イラストレーションは生活に溶け込んで存在しているもの、その視点を大切に描いています。

1967年神奈川県生まれ / 東京都在住 /
女子美術大学芸術学部デザイン科中退

See more artwork(バリエーションはこちら)≫ http://www.pict-web.com/akemi_tezuka

た

007

008

009

010

011

012

013

tetsuro oh!no
tetsuro oh!no

There are things in common with the Japanese soul in the world of modern art. I express various lifestyles through the world of illustration.

モダンインテリアの世界には、"和"の精神と共通するものがあります。様々なライフスタイルをイラストの世界で表現しています。

Media : Photoshop CS2 / Illustrator 10
画材 : Photoshop CS2 / Illustrator 10

See more artwork(バリエーションはこちら) ≫ http://www.pict-web.com/tetsuro_ohno

た

018

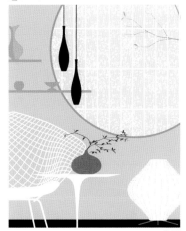

019

020

021

022

023

Michiyo Tokuda
とくだ みちよ

Media : Illustrator 5.5J / Photoshop 5.5 /
Acrylic / Watercolor
画材 : Illustrator 5.5J / Photoshop 5.5 /
アクリル絵の具 / 水彩

I hope to draw illustrations that have vivid colors and a story like a foreign illustration book, while taking care of the texture of material created with pigments.

絵の具で制作した素材の質感を大切に外国の絵本のような色鮮やかでストーリー性のあるイラストを心がけて描いています。

1976年大阪生まれ / 和歌山在住 / 嵯峨美術短期大学卒

See more artwork(バリエーションはこちら)≫ http://www.pict-web.com/michiyo_tokuda

016

010

017

018

019

020

TOKUMA
TOKUMA

Media : Illustrator
画材 : Illustrator

Reducing the formal record to a memory. I'm conscious of expressions that have an afterglow. Sometimes walking in the mountains.

記録から記憶だけに削ぎ落としていくこと。余韻のある表現を意識すること。時々、山を歩くこと。

1973年新潟生まれ / 東京在住 / 広告デザイン専門学校卒

See more artwork（バリエーションはこちら） ≫ http://www.pict-web.com/tokuma

001

002

003

004

た

Kazushi Tokumitsu
徳光 和司

Media : Acrylic gouache / Ink
画材：アクリルガッシュ / インク

Now, when I put together my favorite things, and colors I like, into an casual lifestyle space, my creative juices start flowing.

なにげなく生活している空間に今一番好きなものや好きな色を加えることで創作意欲が湧いてきます。

1963年生まれ / 東京在住 / 日本大学藝術学部美術学科卒

See more artwork（バリエーションはこちら）≫ http://www.pict-web.com/kazushi_tokumitsu

034

035

036

037

038

039

Gaku Nakagawa
中川 学

Media : Pencil / Photoshop 5.0 J /
Illustrator 9.02
画材：鉛筆 / Photoshop 5.0 J / Illustrator 9.02

Not being bound by forcibly bringing out my personality, I want to catch the best form of an object that I ought to draw, and put it on the page.

無理に自分の個性などを出すことに縛られることなく、描くべきものの一番もちのいい形をとらえて画面につなぎとめてゆきたいです。

1966年東京生まれ / 京都在住 / 仏教大学文学部仏教学科卒

See more artwork（バリエーションはこちら）≫ http://www.pict-web.com/gaku_nakagawa

047

051

052

053

054

055

な

Kazuhiro Nakazato
仲里 カズヒロ

Laughing a lot myself, learning about the laughter in the casual everyday, spending time with people who laugh a lot, and then scheming to cause other people to snicker.

自分が多いに笑うこと、何気ない日常から笑いを学ぶこと、よく笑うひとたちと一緒に過ごすこと、そしてクスクス笑わせようと大いに工夫すること。

Media : Illustrator CS / Photoshop CS
画材 : Illustrator CS / Photoshop CS

1964年大阪生まれ / 大阪在住

See more artwork(バリエーションはこちら)≫ http://www.pict-web.com/kazuhiro_nakazato

015

016

017

な

018

019

020

Kana Nakajima
中島 香奈

Media : Pencil / Watercolor pencil
画材：鉛筆 / 水彩色鉛筆

1968年大阪府生まれ /
京都在住 / 大阪モード学園メイクアップスタイリスト科

I want to take care to draw the depth of life and the richness of the heart from the inside, even though it's a bit inconvenient, and it takes a while.

少し不便だったり手間がかかっても、その中から生まれる暮らしの深みや心の豊かさを大切にして描いていきたいです。

な

See more artwork（バリエーションはこちら）≫ http://www.pict-web.com/kana_nakajima

010

009

011

012

013

014

181

Ryoji Nakajima
中島 良二

Media : Acrylic / Craypas
画材：アクリル / クレパス

Sad as if happy, ugly as if beautiful. I aim to draw pictures in which each person who sees them feels without inhibition.

楽しいようで哀しい、美しいようで醜い。見る人それぞれが、自由に感じとれるような絵を心掛けて描いています。

1976年大阪府生まれ / 大阪在住 / 神戸大学人間行動表現学科卒

See more artwork（バリエーションはこちら）≫ http://www.pict-web.com/ryoji_nakajima

001

002

003

004

005

006

な

Yoco Nagamiya
永宮 陽子

Media : Watercolor / Pen
画材：水彩 / ペン

I want to draw women who have a presence of beauty through well trimmed simple lines.

そぎ落とされたシンプルなラインで、存在感ある美しさを持つ女性を描きたいです。

1973年大阪府生まれ / 大阪在住 /
Masa Mode Academy of Art研究科卒

See more artwork(バリエーションはこちら) ≫ http://www.pict-web.com/yoco_nagamiya

055

056

057

058

059

060

な

Michinori Naro
奈路 道程

Media : Acrylic /
Pencil（DERMATOGRAPH:BLACK）/ Collage
画材：アクリル絵具（ターナー）/ ペンシル
（DERMATOGRAPH:BLACK）/ コラージュ

I'm trying to express the characteristics of all of the tools I use to draw.I enjoy thinking about how I bring successes out of failures on the page.

各使用画材の特性が出るように気をつけている。失敗を失敗とせず画面上で成功の方向へどう持っていくかを考えるのが楽しい。

1964年高知県生まれ / 大阪在住 / 別府大学美学美術史学科卒

See more artwork（バリエーションはこちら）≫ http://www.pict-web.com/michinori_naro

033

032

034

035

036

Taichi Nishida
西田 太一

Media : Pencil / Photoshop CS2
画材：鉛筆 / Photoshop CS2

I treasure ideas because through the process of sifting through lots of ideas, works which can communicate with the people who see them, are realized.

アイデアを大切にしています。たくさんのアイデアを出し選別していく過程で、見る人とコミュニケーションをとることのできる作品が仕上がるからです。

1982年愛媛県生まれ / 東京在住 / University College Falmouth卒

See more artwork（バリエーションはこちら）≫ http://www.pict-web.com/taichi_nishida

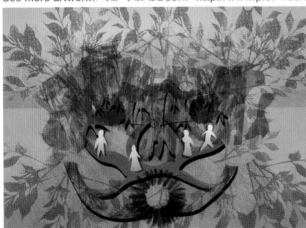

001

002

003

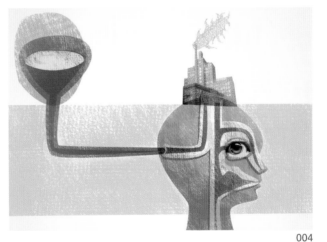

004

005

006

な

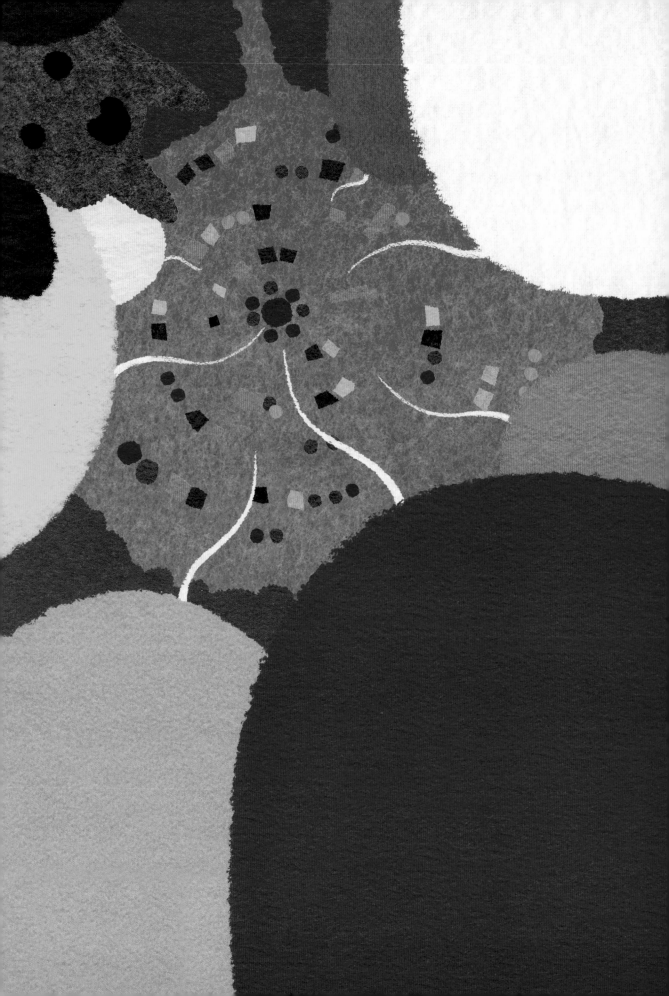

Nu Amu Misin ?
Nu Amu Misin ?

Media : Photoshop CS2 / Illustrator CS2
画材 : Photoshop CS2 / Illustrator CS2

We create illustrations out of dolls that are actually made with the theme of "a continuing tale."

「物語の続き」をテーマに、実際に制作したぬいぐるみをイラスト化しております。

ヌウ アム ミシン ？ / 代表・岩崎一博 / ユイヨシコ / ナゴカオル
1971年東京生まれ / 東京在住 / 東京芸術大学デザイン科卒

See more artwork（バリエーションはこちら）≫ http://www.pict-web.com/nu_amu_misin

な

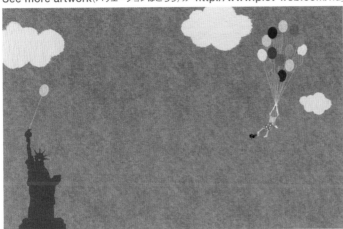

001

002

003

004

005

006

007

008

Yuka Nemoto
根本 有華

Media : Acrylic / Water color / Pastel / Canvas / Paper
画材 : アクリル / 水彩 / パステル / キャンバス / 紙

I want to draw nostalgia and sadness. I mainly work on landscape paintings from the images I see from my car window, but I also work on people, things, and animals, etc. I sometimes use a computer.

懐かしさとせつなさを描きたいです。車窓から見た景色をイメージとする風景画を中心に人、物、動物なども手掛けます。時によりPCも使用。

1975年栃木県生まれ / 東京都在住 / 日本大学芸術学部美術学科卒業

See more artwork(バリエーションはこちら) ≫ http://www.pict-web.com/yuka_nemoto

001

002

003

004

005

193

Akiko Nozaki
のざき あきこ

Media : Photoshop 5.0 / Oil Pastel
画材 : Photoshop 5.0 / オイルパステル

I graduated from the Kuwasawa Design Institute, and started working independently in 2001. My main job as been at Gakken Illustration and Sangetsu Hangings, aside from those I've worked on numerous books. I want to move to draw without getting stuck in any genre.

桑沢デザイン研究所卒業、2001年に独立。主な仕事に Gakken絵本、サンゲツ壁紙、他、書籍等多数で活動中。 ジャンルにとらわれずに描いていきたいと思います。

1974年埼玉県生まれ / 東京在住 / 桑沢デザイン研究所卒

See more artwork（バリエーションはこちら）》 http://www.pict-web.com/akiko_nozaki

009

008

010

011

012

013

な

Noritake
のりたけ

Media : Acrylic / Pencil
画材：アクリル / 鉛筆

I work mainly on editorials and exhibitions. I express a unique world view through motifs of figures, plants and animals, scenes, etc. My anthology is "Daysleeper" (published by Utrecht).

エディトリアル、展覧会を中心に活動を行う。人物、動植物、風景などをモチーフに独自の世界観を表現する。作品集に『Daysleeper』(UTRECHT刊)

1978年岡山県生まれ / 東京在住 / セツ・モードセミナー卒

See more artwork（バリエーションはこちら）≫ http://www.pict-web.com/noritake

001

002

003

004

005

006

Yutaka Hashimoto
橋本 豊

Media : Pen / Chinese ink / Pencil /
Illustrator 10
画材：ペン / 墨汁 / 鉛筆 / Illustrator 10

I think that pictures that are simple and have a tale
are good.

シンプルで、物語のある絵が良いと思っています。

1975年埼玉県生まれ / 東京在住 / 日本大学芸術学部美術学科卒業

See more artwork（バリエーションはこちら）≫ http://www.pict-web.com/yutaka_hashimoto

001

は

002

003

004

005

199

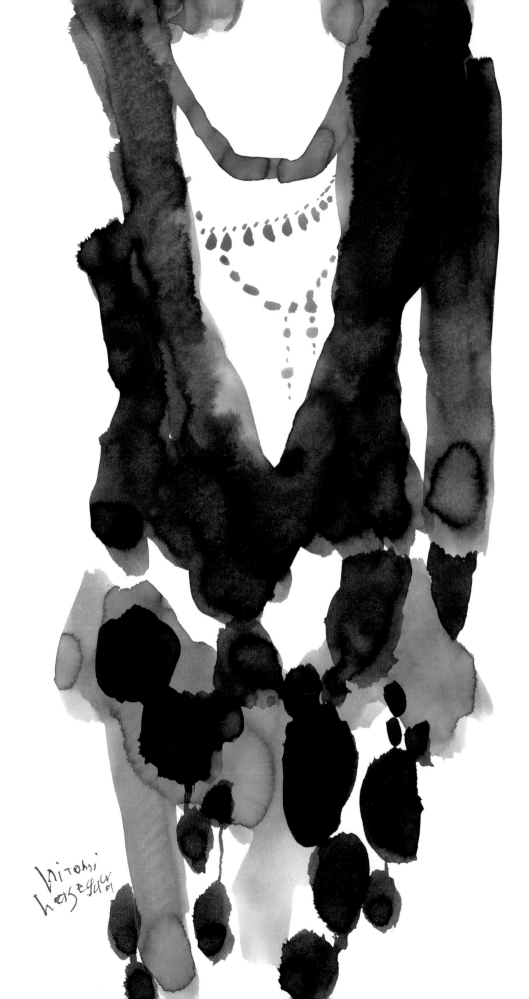

Hitomi Hasegawa
長谷川 ひとみ

Media : Colored ink
画材：カラーインク

Using colors, I draw scenes that catch my eye and the feelings that I have at that time. I'm happy if the people who see my works feel cheery and light.

目に入ってくる風景やそのときの気持ちなどを色にのせて描いています。見る人が、明るく軽やかな気分になってくれれば嬉しいです。

1976年新潟県生まれ / 東京在住 / 長岡造形大学視覚デザイン科卒

See more artwork（バリエーションはこちら）≫ http://www.pict-web.com/hitomi_hasegawa

021

022

023

024

025

026

は

Yoko Hasegawa
長谷川 洋子

Media : Antique lace / Bead / Kimono cloth /
Accessories / Oldmetro ticket / Shell / Old stamp
画材：アンティークレース / ビーズ / 着物生地 /
服飾パーツ / 古メトロ切符 / 貝 / ヴィンテージ切手 etc

The theme is "an amalgamation of nostalgia and
contemporary fresh air." I create, while I take care
to select charming materials that cross national
borders and generations, and to put Japanese
people's pathos in.

テーマは「懐かしさと現代の新鮮な空気を融合」。年
代、国境を超えて魅力的な素材をセレクトする事と、
日本人の情念を込める事を大切にし制作しています。

1981年静岡県生まれ / 多摩美術大学情報デザイン学科卒

See more artwork（バリエーションはこちら）≫ http://www.pict-web.com/yoko_hasegawa

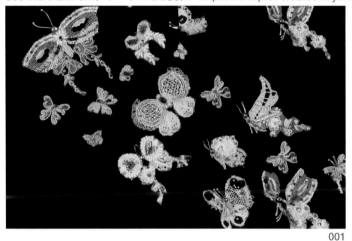

001

002

003

004

005

006

は

203

Asami Hattori
服部 あさ美

Media : Crayon / Pencil
画材：クレヨン / 鉛筆

I draw motifs of water, light, and shade; and people and animals tangled up in them. I hope to express fleeting moments that cannot be grasped in my hands.

水と光と影、そしてそれに絡まる人や動物をモチーフに描いています。自分の手では捕らえることのできない刹那な瞬間を、表現できたらと思います。

1975年神奈川県生まれ / 東京在住

See more artwork（バリエーションはこちら）≫ http://www.pict-web.com/asami_hattori

001

002

003

004

005

は

Motohiro Hayakawa
早川 モトヒロ

Media : Acrylic / Pencil
画材：アクリル絵の具 / 鉛筆

I have the power of imagination, freedom, and poison; cute "Hayakawa" world. American comic books and old American animation, punk rock music, etc.

想像力と自由と毒がありかわいい早川ワールド。アメコミやアメリカなどの昔のアニメ、音楽パンクロック。

1974年山口県生まれ / 東京在住 / 山口芸術短期大学デザイン科卒

See more artwork（バリエーションはこちら）≫ http://www.pict-web.com/motohiro_hayakawa

001

は

002

003

005

005

207

Atsushi Hara
ハラ アツシ

Media : Photoshop 5.5 / Pencil / Gouache
画材 : Photoshop 5.5 / 鉛筆 / ガッシュ

I aim to make illustrations that have not just nostalgia, but also a universality that is popular in any time period.

ノスタルジーだけではない、いつの時代にも通用するような普遍性を持ったイラストレーションを目指しています。

1970年東京都生まれ / 東京在住 / セツ・モード・セミナー卒

See more artwork(バリエーションはこちら) ≫ http://www.pict-web.com/atsushi_hara

001

002

003

004

005

006

は

Rikazu Harada
原田 リカズ

Media : Acrylic gouache / Photoshop CS2 /
Illustrator CS2
画材 : アクリルガッシュ / Photoshop CS2 /
Illustrator CS2

I finish my works with a strong existence, sense, and taste. My strength iscreating things that have a narrative, like scenes in a movie. Not restricting myself to a specific genre, I want to take on a wide range of challenges.

強い存在感とセンス、品を大事にして仕上げています。映画のシーンのような、物語性を含ませるのも得意です。ジャンルを問わず、幅広くチャレンジしたいです。

国立滋賀大学教育学部美術研究室卒

See more artwork(バリエーションはこちら)≫ http://www.pict-web.com/rikazu_harada

002

003

004

005

006

211

Chinatsu Higashi
東 ちなつ

Media : Acrylic gouache / Watercolor / Photoshop 6.0
画材：アクリルガッシュ / 水彩 / Photoshop 6.0

The methods of expressions are various like patterns and paints. That fancy and unique world view is consistent. Recently, I have been seeking new illustrations in which two touches are fused together.

パターン（模様）、ペイントと表現方法は様々。そのファンシーでいて独特な世界観は一貫している。最近はふたつのタッチを融合させた新しいイラストを模索中。

1979年金沢市生まれ / 東京在住 / 日本大学芸術学部卒

See more artwork（バリエーションはこちら）≫ http://www.pict-web.com/chinatsu_higashi

001

002

003

は

004

005

213

ckt (gelyck hy altyts met groote netticheyt en
linghen dede). Dese Tafel op gedaen wesende,
ieu inventie, en ghelyck hy nu ghewoon was, ver-
drooghen in de Sonne, maer of de penneelen niet
lymt en waeren, oft de hitte der Sonnen the
in de vergaderinghen gheborsten, en van
seer t'onvreden, dat zynen arbeydt
m te

Wataru Hikichi
引地 渉

Media : Collage
画材：コラージュ

I create a world that that is "not here, somewhere" through original collages with unconsciously collected kinds of old paper. I cherish analog touch.

無意識に集めてしまう古紙類による独自の貼り絵的コラージュで「ここではないどこか」の世界を創っています。アナログな手触りを大切にしています。

1971年福島県生まれ / 東京在住 / セツ・モードセミナー卒

See more artwork（バリエーションはこちら）》 http://www.pict-web.com/wataru_hikichi

001

002

003

は

005

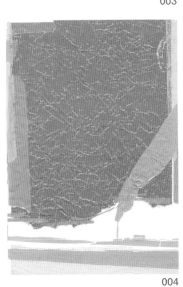

004

Kozue Himi
氷見 こずえ

Media : Fusain / Pastel / Acrylic / Pencil
画材：木炭 / パステル / アクリル / 鉛筆

If I spend ordinary days simply, seriously, and calmly, the feelings in my head will warp in a good way. So I draw them just as they are.

地味に真面目に淡々と平凡な日々を送っていると頭の中がいい感じに歪んでくるので、それをそのまま描いてます。

1976年東京生まれ / 東京在住

See more artwork（バリエーションはこちら）≫ http://www.pict-web.com/kozue_himi

001

002

は

003

004

005

006

007

Keiko Hirasawa
平沢 けいこ

Media : Illustrator8.0
画材 : Illustrator8.0

I want to draw soft translucent women. Also, I hope to express a world where, the people who view my work, can feel happy, even if only a bit.

透明感のあるしなやかな女性を描いていきたいです。そして、見た人が少しでも優しい気持ちになれる様な世界を表現できればと思います。

1970年東京生まれ / 東京在住

See more artwork（バリエーションはこちら）≫ http://www.pict-web.com/keiko_hirasawa

017

018

019

020

021

は

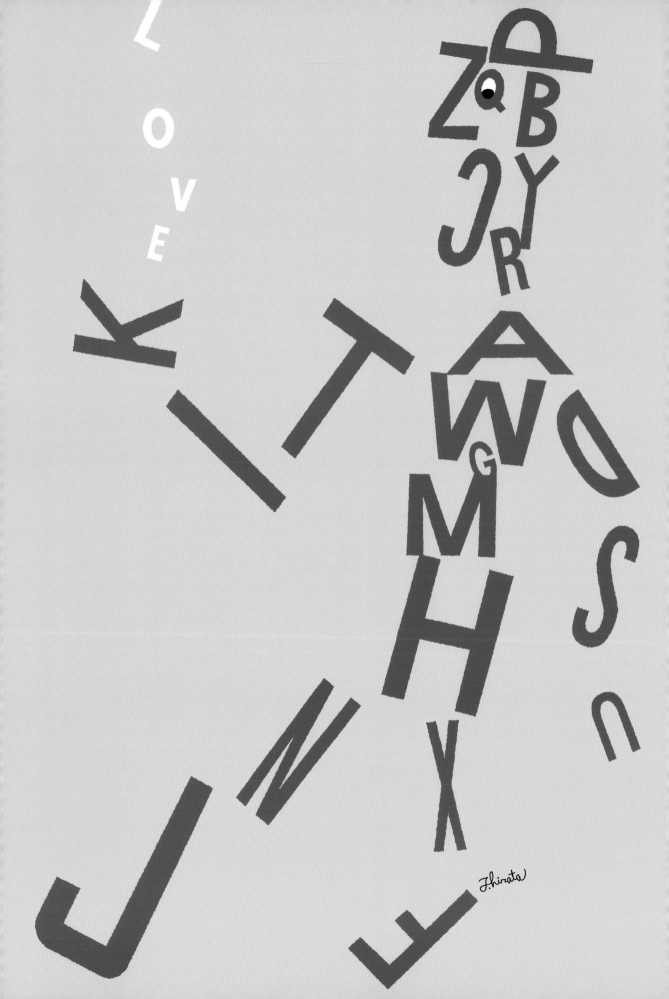

Toshiyuki Hirata
平田 利之

Media : Illustrator CS / Acrylic gouache
画材 : Illustrator CS / アクリルガッシュ

With regard to themes (from economic and politics, to amusement), I'm always dedicated to injecting ideas that have humorous twists, and expressing simple shapes and colors.

テーマ（政治経済から生活娯楽まで）に対して、ユーモアのあるひねりのきいたアイデアを盛り込み、シンプルな色と形で表現することを常に心がけています。

1967年東京生まれ / 東京在住 /
武蔵野美術大学短期大学部デザイン科卒

See more artwork（バリエーションはこちら）≫ http://www.pict-web.com/toshiyuki_hirata

013

014

015

は

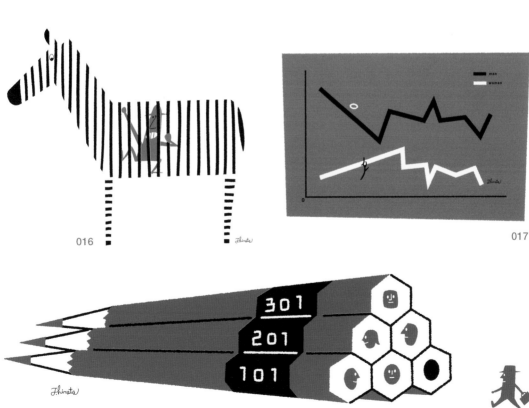

016

017

018

221

Mizue Hirano
平野 瑞恵

Media : Watercolor / Photoshop
画材：水彩 / Photoshop

I take care of the beauty of colors, the transparency, and the tension on the page, a gentle and airy atmosphere that is not too sweet when I draw.

色彩の美しさ、透明感と画面の緊張感、甘くなりすぎずにふんわりと優しい雰囲気を大切に描いています。

1974年兵庫県生まれ / 東京在住 / 多摩美術大学卒

See more artwork（バリエーションはこちら）≫ http://www.pict-web.com/mizue_hirano

001

002

003

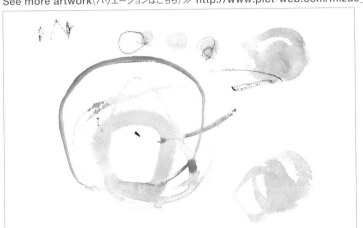

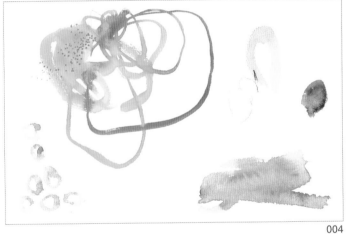

004

005

006

は

Kouichi Hirayama
平山 広一

Media : Ballpoint pen / Marker / Pencil /
PhotoshopCS / Illustrator CS
画材：ポールペン / マーカー / 鉛筆 /
Photoshop CS/Illustrator CS

Expression deeply ties together the deep psyche.
Being my usual self leads to things that only I can
do, and more of it leads to a unique shape in the
world.

表現は深層心理と深く繋がっている。自分らしくある事が、
自分にしか出来ないに繋がり、世界でひとつのカタチへと
繋がっていく。楽しむことが大切だ。

1982年東京生まれ / 東京都多摩市在住 / 片倉高校造形美術コース卒

See more artwork（バリエーションはこちら）≫ http://www.pict-web.com/kouichi_hirayama

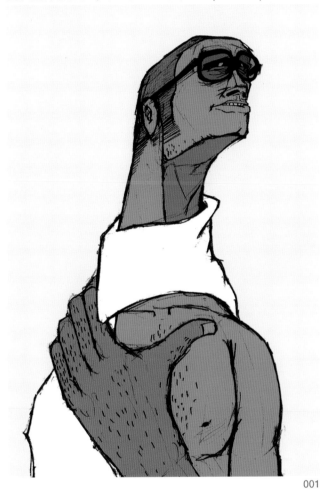

001

002

003

は

004

005

006

225

Sayaka Hirota
廣田 明香

Media : Ink / Acrylic
画材：黒インク / アクリル

1975年京都府生まれ / 東京在住 / 京都精華大学デザイン学科卒

I'm always pursuing compositions that feel good, with the strength and enchantment of life, and curves which are very important to express them.

生命の力強さや艶やかさ、それを表現する上で曲線は非常に重要で、常に気持ちのいい構図を探求しています。

See more artwork（バリエーションはこちら）≫ http://www.pict-web.com/sayaka_hirota

001

002

003

004

005

006

007

は

227

Tetsuya Fukazawa
フカザワ テツヤ

What I would take the most pleasure in, is if I could somehow increase the number of people in the world who imagine, sympathize, and laugh with the world of my expression, and then, if I could somehow contribute to the world.

僕の表現した世界を観て想像したり共感したり笑ってくれる人が増えて、何かしら世の中に貢献する事ができたならそれが僕の一番の喜びです。

Media : Acrylic
画材：アクリル絵の具

1978年生まれ / 東京在住 / イラストレーション青山塾イラストレーション修了

See more artwork（バリエーションはこちら）≫ http://www.pict-web.com/tetsuya_fukazawa

013

014

015

016

017

018

は

Toru Fukuda
福田 透

Media : Illustrator 10 / Photoshop 7.0 /
Painter 7 / Flash MX
画材 : Illustrator 10 / Photoshop 7.0 /
Painter 7 / Flash MX

I want to honestly express things that I'm interest-
ed in and make me happy, regardless of the work. I
find limitless amusement in instincts and whims.

どんな作品にもいま面白がっていること、うれしがっている
ことを素直に表現したいと思っています。直感や思いつき
が面白くてしかたがなくなっています。

1967年兵庫県生まれ / 京都在住/兵庫工業高校デザイン科卒

See more artwork（バリエーションはこちら）≫ http://www.pict-web.com/toru_fukuda

052

053

054

055

056

057

は

231

Yuka Maeda
まえだ ゆか

Media : Photoshop 7.0 / Illustrator 10.0
画材 : Photoshop 7.0 / Illustrator 10.0

I cherish a world view and a presence that comes from expressionlessness. I like the vague feeling that even in sexiness, there remains an innocent atmosphere. I like fashion and trends, so I strain to express fashion, even to the smallest details.

無表情の中に生まれる存在感や世界観を大切にしています。セクシーさの中にもあどけない雰囲気が残るような曖昧な感じが好きです。ファッションやモードが好きなので、ファッションのディティールも細部までこだわって表現しています。

1975年神戸生まれ / 大阪在住

See more artwork（バリエーションはこちら）≫ http://www.pict-web.com/yuka_maeda

001

002

003

004

Noriko Makino
牧野 倫子

Media : Photoshop 6.0 / Illustrator 8.0 /
Painter 6.0J
画材 : Photoshop 6.0 / Illustrator 8.0 /
Painter 6.0J

Outside of work, not falling into a rut, I'm doing whatever I think of freely. Even if it doesn't become a shape, I cherish if there is something to discover.

仕事以外では型にはまらないで、自由に思いつきで何でもやってみるようにしています。形にならなくても何か発見があれば大事にしたいです。

1973年神奈川県生まれ / 神奈川在住 / 多摩美術大学デザイン科卒

See more artwork(バリエーションはこちら)≫ http://www.pict-web.com/noriko_makino

001

002

003

004

005

MagmaGiants
マグマ ジャイアンツ

Media : Pencil / Acrylic / Crayon /
Chacoal Pen / printer / Photoshop 7
画材：えんぴつ / アクリル / クレヨン /
チャコールペン / プリンター / Photoshop7

When I'm drinking, good ideas float by unexpect-edly. But the drawings that I make when I'm drunk, are really bad when I look at them the next day. From now on, I want to put all my power into every match like a high school baseball player.

呑んでる時、意外といいアイデアが浮かびます。でも酔って描いた絵を次の日見るとほんとひどいです。今後は高校球児のように一戦ごと燃え尽きたいです。

1969年岩手県生まれ / 東京在住 / 桑沢デザイン研究所ビジュアルデザイン科卒

See more artwork（バリエーションはこちら）≫ http://www.pict-web.com/magma_giants

015

016

017

018

019

020

ま

237

Asako Masunouchi
升ノ内 朝子

I want to express something like beauty, humour, melancholy and nostalgia, hidden in everyday life. I mainly work in Japan, UK, France and Greece.

日常生活の中の、ちょっとしたおかしみや懐かしみのある風景を描いています。日本、イギリス、フランス、ギリシャと国を問わず活動しています。

Media : Acrylic / Colorpencil / Photoshop CS
画材：アクリル / 色鉛筆 / Photoshop CS

1977年東京都生まれ / 千葉在住 /
University of Brighton イラストレーション科卒

See more artwork（バリエーションはこちら）≫ http://www.pict-web.com/asako_masunouchi

023

024

025

026

027

028

MACHIKO
MACHIKO

Media : Photoshop 7.0 / Illustrator 10.0
画材 : Photoshop 7.0 / Illustrator 10.0

I create being conscious of a sense like not too sweet bitter chocolate, something a bit poisonous, the toughness, and the subtractive design that is in a woman.

甘すぎないビターチョコのような感覚、少し毒のあるもの、女性の中にあるしたたかさ、引き算のデザインを意識して創作しています。

1983年神奈川生まれ / 兵庫在住 / 美術系専門学校グラフィックデザイン専科卒

See more artwork(バリエーションはこちら) ≫ http://www.pict-web.com/machiko

001

002

003

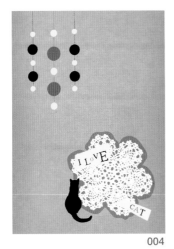

004

005

006

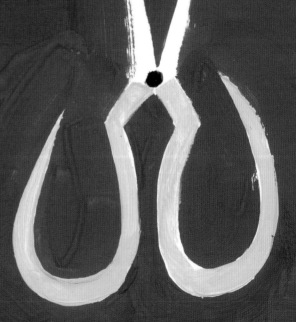

mode
de France

FABRICATION FRANÇAIS

UNE
GROSSE / 6 // 156 // 156 //

Miyuki Matsuo
松尾 ミユキ

Media : Acrylic / Oilpastel / Coupy
画材：アクリル / オイルパステル / クーピー

I get inspiration from the casual shapes and colors around me that I see in everyday life.

日常生活のなかで目にする、身の回りにある何気ないもののかたちや色からインスピレーションを受けている。

1973年名古屋生まれ / 東京在住 / パレットクラブ京都校卒

See more artwork（バリエーションはこちら）》 http://www.pict-web.com/miyuki_matsuo

001

002

003

ま

004

005

243

Satoshi Matsuzawa
マツザワ サトシ

Media : Mechanical pencil / Illustrator 8.0 /
Photoshop 4.0
画材：シャープペンシル / Illustrator 8.0 /
Photoshop 4.0

The expression and mood that humans encapsulate. Each person has a presence; sound and aroma is released... I aim to express that human portrait.

人間が生みだす表情や空気感。それぞれの空気を纏（まと）い、音を放ち、更には香りを放つ・・・そんな人物像の表現を目指しています。

1967年大坂府生まれ / 栃木県在住 / 青山学院大学卒

See more artwork（バリエーションはこちら）≫ http://www.pict-web.com/satoshi_matsuzawa

012

013

014

015

016

017

Manabu Matsuda
松田 学

Media : Illustrator 8.0
画材 : Illustrator 8.0

I want to draw scenes where people that see them can return to a moment in the past and say "that's it, that's it". I also want to try to do book binding work.

見る人が「こんな事あった、あった」と一瞬過去に戻れるようなシーンを描いていきたいと思っています。装幀のお仕事してみたいです。

1968年大阪府生まれ / 大阪在住 / 大阪芸術大学デザイン学科卒

See more artwork(バリエーションはこちら)≫ http://www.pict-web.com/manabu_matsuda

031

032

033

034

035

036

Shiho Matsubara
松原 シホ

Media : Illustrator 10.0
画材 : Illustrator 10.0

I create, conscious of sophisticated people, sur-face color, and balance of form. I'm happy if I can bring out a somewhat subtle airiness.

色面・フォルムのバランス、ヌケのいい人々を意識して製作しています。なんだか微妙な空気感が出せていると嬉しいです。

1971年東京生まれ / 東京在住 / 早稲田大学政治経済学部政治学科卒

See more artwork (バリエーションはこちら) ≫ http://www.pict-web.com/shiho_matsubara

031

032

033

034

035

036

037

ま

Mariko Matsumoto
松元 まり子

Media : Pencil / Photoshop Elements / Crayon
/ Colorpencil / Marker / Pen / Watercolor
画材：鉛筆 / Photoshop Elements / クレヨン /
色鉛筆 / マーカー / ペン / 水彩

Thinking about clothes to dress people in is something I enjoy, but sometimes I get carried away.
Not only clothes, but also the relationship between
colors is something I want to give a lot of thought
too.

人物にどういう服を着せるかを考えるのは一つの楽しみな
のですが、悩む所でもあります。服にかぎらず、色と色との
関係を大切に考えたいと思います。

1967年名古屋生まれ / 名古屋在住 / セツ・モードセミナー卒

See more artwork（バリエーションはこちら）≫ http://www.pict-web.com/mariko_matsumoto

045

046

047

048

049

ま

Satoshi Maruyama
丸山 誠司

Media : Oil Pastel / Acrylic
画材：オイルパステル / アクリル絵具

1968年岐阜県生まれ / 東京在住 / Masa Mode Academy of Art卒

The way to make a work of art is to not forget humor, and to bring out a living picture.

作品を創作するうえで大切にしていることは、ユーモアを忘れないことと、生きた絵になること。

See more artwork（バリエーションはこちら）≫ http://www.pict-web.com/satoshi_maruyama

001

002

003

004

005

006

007

ま

micca
micca

Media : Watercolor / Acrylic / Pencil
画材：水彩 / アクリル / 鉛筆

I take care with the space that is created around what I draw. I want to make space that changes the atmosphere every time that letters or people's line of sight join it.

紙に何かを描くことで出来る空間を大切にしています。人の目線や文字が加わっていく、そのときどきで雰囲気が変わるような隙間を作っておきたいと思っています。

1976年三重県生まれ / 東京在住 / 京都精華大学美術学部卒

See more artwork (バリエーションはこちら) ≫ http://www.pict-web.com/micca

023

024

025

026

027

Satomi Mizuuchi
みずうち さとみ

Media : gauze / embroidery thread / Paints for fablics
画材：ガーゼ / 刺しゅう糸 / 布描き絵具

I think it's enough and a good success if the people who see the work that I put out smile. I want to continue to draw "loose" pictures with handmade gauze embroidery.

私が創り出すもので見る人が笑顔になってくれたらそれで充分、それで上出来だと思っています。ガーゼに手刺しゅうで"ゆるい"絵を描き続けたいです。

1972年埼玉生まれ / 東京在住 / セツ・モードセミナー卒

See more artwork（バリエーションはこちら）≫ http://www.pict-web.com/satomi_mizuuchi

001

002

003

004

005

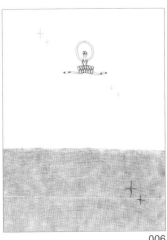

006

Kenichiro Mizuno
水野 健一郎

Media : Photoshop 7.0
画材 : Photoshop 7.0

In order to declare the self, hidden in the depth of superficial technique the composition's gestalt is deliberately amorphous. Stroll through scenery in my mind, seeking the romanticism vacilating between deja vu and jamais vu.

表面的な手法の奥底に潜む自我を表明するため作品の形態はあえて不定形。既視感と未視感の狭間にゆれるロマンチシズムを求めて脳内風景を散策中。

1967年岐阜県生まれ / 東京在住 / セツ・モードセミナー卒

See more artwork(バリエーションはこちら)≫ http://www.pict-web.com/kenichiro_mizuno

001

002

003

ま

004

005

006

259

Akiko Miyakoshi
宮越 暁子

Media : Color Paper / Incense Stick / Ink/
Ceramic Stucco
画材：色紙 / 線香 / インク / セラミックスタッコ

The beauty of color, the texture of analog.
色のきれいさ、アナログの質感。

1982年埼玉県生まれ / 茨城県在住 /
武蔵野美術大学視覚伝達デザイン学科卒

See more artwork(バリエーションはこちら) ≫ http://www.pict-web.com/akiko_miyakoshi

001

002

003

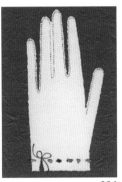

004

005

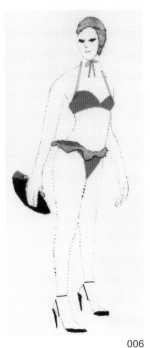

006

007

ま

Aki Miyajima
宮島 亜希

Media : Ballpoint Pen / Pigmen t/ Chinese Ink
画材：水性ボールペン / 鉛筆 / 顔彩 / 墨汁

The first thing I understand is that a woman has a core strength, an interior beauty. By drawing them, I want not only women, but also men to feel the "feminine".

女性が持っている、芯の強さ、内面の美しさを、自分自身が一番に理解し、描き出すことで、女性にも男性にも「女らしさ」を感じてもらいたいです。

1979年滋賀県生まれ / 東京在住 /
京都芸術デザイン専門学校デザイン総合学科卒

See more artwork（バリエーションはこちら）≫ http://www.pict-web.com/aki_miyajima

046

047

048

049

050

051

Jiro Miyata
ミヤタ ジロウ

Media : Illustrator 10.0
画材 : Illustrator 10.0

I create while thinking about the seasons and the light involved in them. Ideas float by when I'm taking a walk, or idly listening to music.

季節や、それに伴う光について考えながら制作しています。散歩している時や、音楽をぼんやり聴いている時に、アイデアが浮かんだりします。

1972年大阪府生まれ / 大阪在住

See more artwork（バリエーションはこちら）≫ http://www.pict-web.com/jiro_miyata

027

028

029

030

031

032

Akihiro Morita
森田 明宏

Media : Photoshop 6 / Pencil
画材 : Photoshop 6 / 鉛筆

Inspiration comes from various things. They are the element of letters, buildings, clothing, and also people facial expressions.

インスピレーションは様々な物から受けます。それは文字のエレメントであったり、建物や服、人の表情であったりもします。

1981年大阪府生まれ / 東京在住 /
大阪芸術大学ビジュアルデザイン学科卒

See more artwork（バリエーションはこちら）≫ http://www.pict-web.com/akihiro_morita

001

002

ま

003

Toru Morooka
師岡 とおる

Media : Photoshop CS / Illustrator CS / Pencil / Pen / Embroidery thread / Fabric / Silkscreen
画材 : Photoshop CS / Illustrator CS / 鉛筆 / ペン / 刺繍糸 / 布 / シルクスクリーン

I create play.

遊びにする。

1972年東京生まれ / 東京在住 /
武蔵野美術大学空間演出デザイン学科卒

See more artwork（バリエーションはこちら）≫ http://www.pict-web.com/toru_morooka

001

002

003

004

ま

Emi Yamaguchi
山口 絵美

Media : Illustrator 8.0
画材 : Illustrator 8.0

Through my own filter, I hope to express the excitement in everyday casual movement with happiness and good feeling.

日常の何げない動作のおもしろさを、自分のフィルターを通してたのしく、気持ちよく表現したいと思っています。

1971年東京都生まれ / 東京在住 / 青山学院女子短大芸術学科卒

See more artwork(バリエーションはこちら) ≫ http://www.pict-web.com/emi_yamaguchi

047

048

049

050

051

052

053

や

Mariko Yamazaki
山崎 真理子

Continuing to stimulate myself all the time. What I actually take care to do before I create an work, is to collect information and observe. I'm dedicated to realistic distortions.

常に自分に刺激を与え続けること。実際に作品を描くうえで大切にしていることは、資料収集と観察。リアリティーのあるデフォルメ表現を心がけています。

Media : Illustrator 8.0
画材 : Illustrator 8.0

1975年大阪生まれ / 大阪在住 /
大阪デザイナー専門学校グラフィックデザイン科卒

See more artwork(バリエーションはこちら) ≫ http://www.pict-web.com/mariko_yamazaki

008

010

011

012

013

009

や

Nobuo Yamada
山田 ノブオ

Media : Flash 4 / Illustrator 8.0.2 /
Photoshop 6.0
画材 : Flash 4 / Illustrator 8.0.2 / Photoshop 6.0

My thought is based a rhythm's mind-blowing feeling that is produced when a few uplifting colors I picked out are repeated. Recently I have been enjoying the allure of perspective through gradations.

ピックアップした幾つかの色を、反復させることで生じるリズムの恍惚感が根っこにあります。最近はグラデーションによる視点の誘惑が楽しい。

1962年東京都生まれ / 東京在住 / 阿佐ヶ谷美術専門学校卒

See more artwork（バリエーションはこちら）》 http://www.pict-web.com/nobuo_yamada

040

043

044

041

042

045

や

Shigeya Yamamoto
山本 重也

Media : Watercolor
画材：水彩

I like to express catching light and shadow through watercolors. This time, I symbolically express the form brought out by the human body. In order to do this I use the colors in a simple manner.

水彩で光と影を捉える表現が好きです。今回は人体が作り出す形を象徴的に表現してみました。そのため色も簡素にしています。

1964年大阪府生まれ / 東京在住 / 大阪デザイナー専門学校中退

See more artwork（バリエーションはこちら）≫ http://www.pict-web.com/shigeya_yamamoto

029

030

031

032

033

034

Yuko Yamamoto
山本 祐布子

Media : Paper
画材：紙

The image that I catch in the beginning, I really try to hold onto it. I think about how the painting flows so it feels good on paper. The form. The colors. The texture. After these things I just leave it up to my hands.

最初につかまえたイメージを、きちんとつかまえておくこと。紙面の中で、絵がどういうふうに流れたら気持ちがよいかを考えること。形。色彩。質感。あとは、手のまかせるままに、するだけです。

1977年東京生まれ / 東京在住 / 京都精華大学デザイン科卒

See more artwork（バリエーションはこちら）≫ http://www.pict-web.com/yuko _yamamoto

007

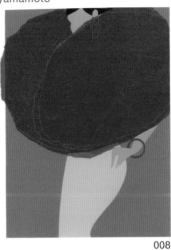

008

009

010

011

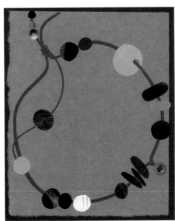

012

Naomi Yuge
弓削 ナオミ

Media : Photoshop 7.0 / Illustrator 10.0 /
Chinese pen / Pencil
画材 : Photoshop 7.0 / Illustrator 10.0 / 筆ペン /
鉛筆

When I create a work: what I deeply value drawing
on my perspective as a woman, I want to express
lifestyles, situations, and a feeling of gentle happiness that arouses one's sympathies.

女性の観点から共感を呼ぶライフスタイルやシチュエーシ
ョン、やさしいシアワセ感を表現したいと意識しています。

1971年大阪府生まれ / 大阪在住 /
京都芸術短期大学ビジュアルデザイン学科卒

See more artwork（バリエーションはこちら）》 http://www.pict-web.com/naomi_yuge

039

040

041

042

043

Yutakana
ユタカナ

Media : Color pencil / Pencil
画材：色鉛筆／鉛筆

Everyday, I create exciting works straightforwardly and cheerfully, things that are at their heart made by drawing vivid lines that have movement.

生き生きした線を描くことでワクワクするような動きのある作品をつくることを根底に日々まっすぐ楽しく制作活動をしています。

1976年滋賀県生まれ／東京在住／大阪デザイナー専門学校卒

See more artwork（バリエーションはこちら）≫ http://www.pict-web.com/yutakana

020

021

023

024

025

026

や

Yurikov Kawahiro
ユリコフ・カワヒロ

I want to draw drama from wherever I see it. I want to put comic elements into even sad scenes, that make you snicker when you catch a glimpse of them.

どこかで目にする様なドラマを描きたい。悲しいシーンでも、端から見たらクスっと笑える、喜劇的な要素を入れたい。

Media : Pencil / Copier / Photoshop CS2
画材：鉛筆 / モノクロコピー / Photoshop CS2

1981年生まれ / 京都在住 / 京都造形芸術大学情報デザイン学科卒

See more artwork（バリエーションはこちら）≫ http://www.pict-web.com/yurikov_kawahiro

026

025

027

028

029

030

や

Yocotino
ヨーコチーノ

I lightly draw female celebrities' daily life with humor while enjoying myself.

セレブな女の子の日常を軽やかにユーモアを持って、自分自身楽しみながら描くことです。

Media : Pen / Watercolor
画材：ペン / 水彩

1973年大阪府生まれ / 大阪在住 /
Masa Mode Academy of Art研究科卒

See more artwork（バリエーションはこちら）≫ http://www.pict-web.com/yocotino

001

002

003

004

005

や

Kaori Yoshioka
吉岡 香織

I want to draw woman so that people can smell their aroma.

香りが感じられる女性を描きたいです。

Media : Photoshop 6.0 / Chinese Ink / Color Ink
画材 : Photoshop 6.0 / 墨汁 / カラーインク

1974年広島県生まれ / 東京在住 / 文化服装学院メンズデザインコース卒

See more artwork(バリエーションはこちら) ≫ http://www.pict-web.com/kaori_yoshioka

001

002

003

004

005

006

289

Yuko Yoshioka
吉岡 ゆうこ

Media : Photoshop 7.0 / Pencil
画材 : Photoshop 7.0 / 鉛筆他

I hope to draw illustrations that seem to have a "space and openness" that the imagination of the people who see them can enter. Furthermore my futureaim is to make thick beautiful things after I get on both sides of things like "beauty / ugliness" "goodness / badness," etc. ponder, and understand them.

見る人の想像力が入れる『余裕/隙間』を持つイラストを描きたい。さらに『善/悪』『美/醜』などの両極面を咀嚼し、厚みのある美しいものを創っていく事が今後の目標。

1972年東京生まれ / 武蔵野美術短期大学空間演出デザインコース卒業

See more artwork(バリエーションはこちら) ≫ http://www.pict-web.com/yuko_yoshioka

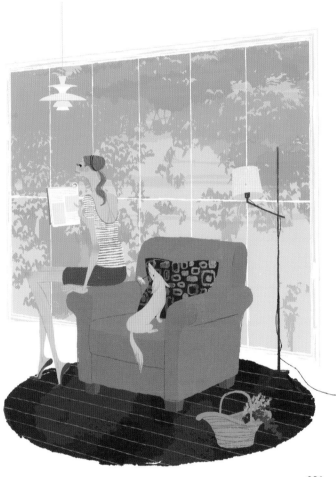

031

032

033

034

035

036

や

Megumi Yoshizane
吉實 恵

Media : Liquitex / Watercolor
画材：リキテックス／水彩絵の具

I draw when I feel a mysterious power in something close to me like scenes,animals, figures, etc. I hope I can share that sensation with lots of people.

風景、動物、人物など、身近で見慣れた存在に神秘的な力を感じて描いています。そんな感覚を、多くの人と共有できたらいいなと思っています。

1970年千葉生まれ／東京在住／
武蔵野美術大学視覚伝達デザイン学科卒

See more artwork（バリエーションはこちら）≫ http://www.pict-web.com/megumi_yoshizane

001

002

003

004

005

006

や

Takeshi Yonemochi
米持 岳士

Media : Photoshop 7.0
画材 : Photoshop 7.0

Airing out the influences (fashion, games) I've had until now that have passed through me.

今まで受けて来た影響(ファッション、ゲーム)を私を通して吐き出す事。

1978年新潟県生まれ / 東京都在住 / 独学

See more artwork(バリエーションはこちら)≫ http://www.pict-web.com/takeshi_yonemochi

001

002

003

004

や

Kazushi Ryoguchi
両口 和史

Media : Illustrator 8.0
画材 : Illustrator 8.0

The atmosphere of the 60s and 70s that I felt in real time when I was a kid. I want to express the nostalgia of that time, and the air that I like so much, coupled with illustrations that have a moderntaste.

子供の頃にリアルタイムで感じた60〜70年代の雰囲気。あの大好きだった懐かしい時間と空気を、モダンなテイストのイラストに加味して表現していきたいです。

1967年京都市生まれ/ 滋賀在住 /
京都精華大学美術学部ビジュアル コミュニケーション デザイン学科卒

See more artwork（バリエーションはこちら）≫ http://www.pict-web.com/kazushi_ryoguchi

023

024

025

026

020

022

019

ら

room-composite
room-composite

A design unit centered around art director and graphic designer TOMOYA KAISHI. We are always pondering new forms of communication.

アートディレクター / グラフィックデザイナーのカイシトモヤを中心としたデザインユニット。新しいコミュニケーションのカタチを常に思案中。

Media : Photoshop CS / Illustrator CS
画材 : Photoshop CS / Illustrator CS

1975年兵庫県生まれ / 東京在住 / 大阪デザイナー専門学校卒

See more artwork（バリエーションはこちら）≫ http://www.pict-web.com/room_composite

001

002

003

004

005

006

Miki Rezai
レザイ 美樹

Media : Pencil / Pen / Photoshop / Illustrator
画材：鉛筆 / ペン / Photoshop / Illustrator

I draw characters and personalities that naturally cause one to grin while I myself grin. I make use of a graphic designers point of view in my work.

「ニヤリ」としてしまう様なクセのあるキャラクターや人物を、「ニヤリ」としながら描いています。グラフィックデザイナー的視点を生かして制作しています。

1976年埼玉県生まれ / 東京在住 /
多摩美術大学造形表現学部デザイン科卒

See more artwork（バリエーションはこちら）≫ http://www.pict-web.com/miki_rezai

001

002

003

004

005

006

ら

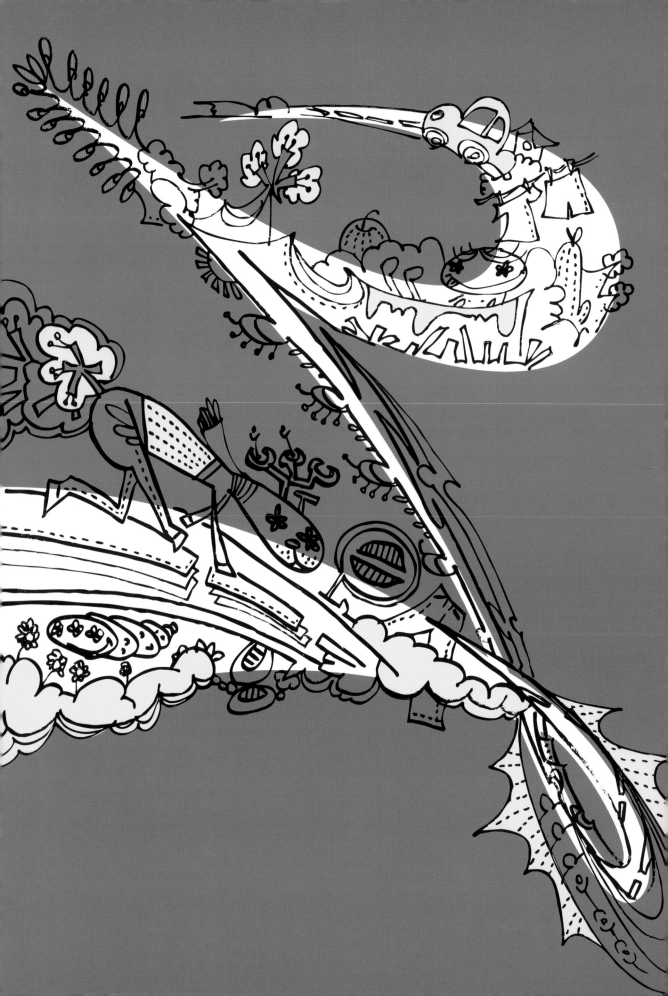

Akira Wakui
ワクイ アキラ

Media : Photoshop CS2 / Illustrator CS2 /
Chinese pen / Acrylic
画材：Photoshop CS2 / Illustrator CS2 /
筆ペン / アクリル絵具

I hope to make lines, colors, and forms that make
people happy when they see them.

見たら楽しくてHAPPYな気分になれるような線、色、形を
描きたいと思っています。

1976年長野県生まれ / 大阪在住 / 京都精華大学デザイン学科卒

See more artwork（バリエーションはこちら） ≫ http://www.pict-web.com/akira_wakui

030

031

032

033

034

035

わ

Noriko Watanabe
渡辺 宣子

I put pigments onto white paper, and carefully paint; for example the kind of feeling I get after I see a movie, and I feel I can't find the words.

例えば、映画を観たあとに残る言葉にできないような気持ちを、白い紙に絵の具をのせて大切に塗り込んでいます。

Media : Liquitex / Watson's paper
画材：使用画材 / リキテックス（アクリル絵の具）/ ワトソン紙

1972年石川県生まれ／東京在住／パレットクラブ卒

See more artwork（バリエーションはこちら）≫ http://www.pict-web.com/noriko_watanabe

001

002

003

004

005

006

Motomu Watanabe
ワタナベ モトム

Media : Photoshop 5.5 / Illustrator 9.0.2
画材 : Photoshop 5.5 / Illustrator 9.0.2

I want to draw dull, cool illustrations. I'm happy if I can somehow bring out feelings that seem aloof and grownup and also bring out a bit of painfully sad feelings.

ショボカッコイイイラストを描いていきたいのです。クールな大人っぽさ、それに少しのせつなさなんかを出せると嬉しいのです。

1971年東京生まれ / 東京在住 / 町田デザイン専門学校卒

See more artwork（バリエーションはこちら）≫ http://www.pict-web.com/motomu_watanabe

013

014

015

016

017

018

Romi Watanabe
わたなべ ろみ

Media : Acrylic / Pen / Color pencil / Ink
画材：アクリル / ペン / 色鉛筆 / インク

I remember things that I saw and was moved by on a journey or in everyday life, and then I draw them when the time is ripe inside me. There are also things I suddenly feel I want to draw. When that happens, I draw at a time when those feelings are strong.

日常や旅先で見て感動したものを憶えていて自分の中で満を持した時に描く。突然描きたくなるものもあるので、そういう時は思いが強い時に描く。

東京在住 / セツ・モードセミナー卒

See more artwork（バリエーションはこちら）≫ http://www.pict-web.com/romi_watanabe

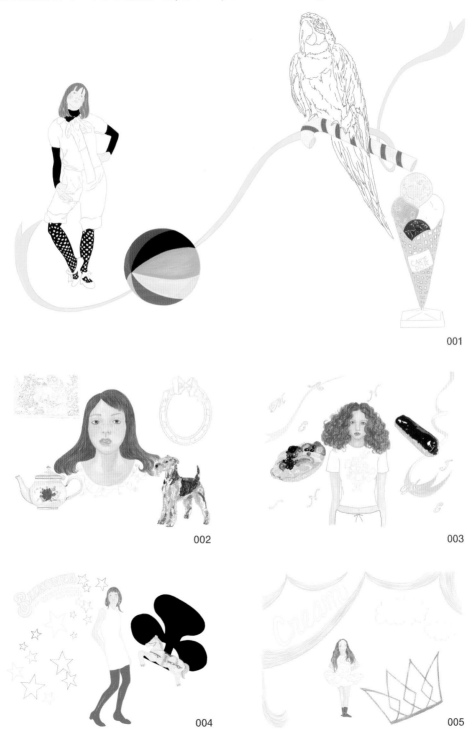

001

002

003

004

005

わ

今、欲しいイラストが見つかる。レンタルもオーダーもできる。

You can find the illustration you are just about looking for.

ピクトのシステム System of pict

Illustration Book Proと連動、
最新の情報をお届けするPICT-WEB.COM

Illustration Book Pro works with PICT-WEB.COM where latest information is available.

Illustration Book Pro

PICT-WEB.COM

Illustration Book Proに掲載されているイラストレーターの作品バリエーション、詳細なプロフィール、カンプデータなど、PICT-WEB.COMに全て掲載されています。

PICT-WEB.COM shows further details such as profiles, comp data and more illustrations.

カンプデータダウンロード
無料メンバー登録受付中!

ストックイラストのレンタル Rights managed stock illustrations

Illustration Book Pro、PICT-WEB.COMに掲載されている
全てのイラストはストックイラストとして、レンタル使用が可能です。

All illustrations in Illustration Book Pro or PICT-WEB.COM can be rented.

イラストレーター名
Illustrator's name

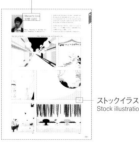

ストックイラスト番号
Stock illustration number

イラストレーター名
Illustrator's name

ストックイラスト番号
Stock illustration number

ご注文方法 Stock Illustration order procedure

お問合せ
Order by call or e-mail

お電話、メール等にてご希望のイラストレーター&ストックイラスト番号をお伝えください。
Please give the name of the illustrator and illustration number.

イラストレーターへの打診
Getting permission

使用の可否をイラストレーターへ打診し、早急にお返事いたします。
You will be informed by PICT once the use of illustration is permitted by the illustrator.

納品
Delivery

データにて納品いたします。
(ファイルダウンロード、メール送信等など臨機応変に対応いたします。)
The illustration will be delivered by e-mail
(attachment or download).

使用料金・許諾について Prices・Permission

使用料金はPICT-WEB.COMのプライスリストをご確認いただくか、お電話にてお気軽にお問合せください。海外での使用料金は別途御見積りいたしますので、お問合せください。
Stock illustration price will be given upon receiving a request information.

掲載作品のレンタルは各イラストレーターの許諾が必要となります。イラストレーターの意向やバッティング等の理由でレンタルできない場合がございますので、ご使用を検討される際（プレゼンテーション前）に必ずお問合せください。
To rent illustrations requires illustrators' permission. Please be sure to inquire the availability of the illustration before giving presentation to your clients. Illustrations may not be available due to illustrators' policy or current position

お問合せ Contact

日本 & アジア Japan and Asia

info@pict-web.com

東日本担当：アスタリスク asterisk
TEL 03-5766-4625

西日本担当：ヴィジョントラック vision track
TEL 06-6316-7363

ピクトはイラストエージェンシーのアスタリスクとヴィジョントラックが共同で
運営するストックイラストとイラストレーターマネジメントのブランドです。
PICT is a management agency of stock illustration and illustrators,
run by the illustration agencies, asterisk and visiontrack.

ヨーロッパ & アメリカ Europe and America

uk@pict-web.com

Europe and America Operating agency:Dutch Uncle
TEL 0044(0)20-7336-7696
Studio Two 16-24 Underwood Street London N1 7JQ
*Dutch Uncle is a creative management agency with offices in London and Copenhagen.

オリジナルイラストのオーダー Special illustration order

Illustration Book Pro、PICT-WEB.COMに掲載されている
全てのイラストレーターはオリジナルイラストの制作受注が可能です。

Special illustration can be requested to any illustrators from Illustration Book Pro or PICT-WEB.COM.

ご注文方法 Special illustration order procedure

お問合せ
Order by call or e-mail

お電話、メール等にて希望イラストレーター、
制作内容等をお伝えください。
Please give the requested illustrator name and
the details of your project.

イラストレーターへの打診
Getting illustrator approval

スケジュール、バッティング等、
受注の可否を確認いたします。
PICT checks with the illustrator his/her schedule
and the current position.

お見積り
Quotation

制作内容、使用媒体、期間等により
お見積りいたします。
Quotation will be given after the exposure
(media/ frequency/ term etc.) is studied.

打合せ
Meetings

原則的にはPICTのスタッフが打合せいたします。
※状況によりイラストレーターも同行いたします。
Details of the illustration will be discussed.

ラフスケッチ提出&確認
Rough draft and confirmation

着色完成前にラフスケッチで
内容をご確認いただきます。
You will check the rough draft.

納品
Delivery

原画、もしくはデータにて納品いたします。
(直接のお届け、発送、ファイルダウンロードなど臨機応変に対応いたします。)
The original illustration or its data will be delivered.

PICT-WEB.COM サイト紹介

Illustration Book Proと連動、
最新の情報をお届けするPICT-WEB.COM

Illustration Book Pro works with PICT-WEB.COM where latest information is available.

Top

欲しいイラストがすぐ見つかる。

Easy access to the exact illustration you are looking for.

PICT-WEB.COMでは本誌掲載を含む200名以上のイラストレーターの最新作がご覧いただけます。イラスト専門エージェンシーとしての経験を生かした、ファッション、インテリアなどのカテゴリー検索の他、タッチ別検索、サムネイル検索といった優れた検索性で、欲しいイラストがすぐに見つかります。

You can view the latest illustrations of over 200 illustrators including all from Illustration Book Pro on PICT-WEB.COM.
From our database, you can search not only by category such as fashion, interior etc., the illustration can be searched also by medium and thumbnails.

A page of illustrator

最新のイラストが続々アップ。

The latest illustration is constantly added.

各イラストレーターのページでは、本書掲載以外のバリエーションイラストを多数掲載。さらにイラストレーターから届く最新のストックイラストを続々アップ。また、詳細なプロフィールや仕事実績など、最新情報をお届けしています。

You can always check the latest illustrations
on their pages adding to the archives.
The page also shows the up-dated work history and profiles.

Coordination service

イラストのコーディネートも。

Coordination support

イラストディレクションにおいて高いスキル、実績をもつピクトの専門コーディネーターに、イラストレーターのコーディネートを依頼することも可能です。プロジェクトに応じたイラストレーターのピックアップ、ストックイラストの検索代行を無料で承ります。豊富な経験、幅広いネットワークを持つピクトのコーディネートサービスをぜひご活用ください。

Our highly skilled staffs can support your requirement
with their own kind of network and experience.

その他にもイラストに関する様々なサービス、コンテンツがございます。ぜひアクセスしてください。
Please access our website for more information and service.

作品貸出し及び使用規定 必ずお読み下さい

貸出使用条件

掲載作品のご使用には作家の許諾が必要となります。作家の意向やバッティング等の理由でお貸出しできない場合がございますので、ご使用を検討される際に必ず弊社へお問い合わせ下さい。作品は「1社1号1版1種1回」限りの使用条件で貸出しております。作品使用料金には作品の独占や所有などの権利は含まれておりません。使用決定された貸出作品と同一又は類似の作品が他社又は他のクライアントで既に使用された、あるいは将来使用される可能性があることをご了承下さい。

作品の貸出から返却まで

貸出作品のご検討期間は貸出日より2週間となっております。検討期間延長の際は必ずご連絡下さい。貸出作品はご使用が決定されましたら即時弊社までご連絡下さい。貸出作品はご使用後、データの消去（ハードディスクへコピーされている場合）を確実に行っていただき、その旨弊社まで必ずご報告下さい。各種メディアにてお貸出をしている場合もデータの消去（ハードディスクへコピーされている場合）を確実に行っていただいた後、貸出票とともにご返却下さい。貸出作品が未使用の場合も使用時と同様の処理を行って下さい。

作品使用料のお支払い

作品使用の決定時に使用料金確認の上、請求書を送付させていただきます。納品書が必要な場合や専用伝票での処理をご希望される場合は前もってお伝え下さい。お支払い方法は請求後60日以内に銀行振込にてお願いいたします。なお、手形によるお支払いはお受けいたしかねます。

キャンセル

作品使用のキャンセルは使用決定の連絡から2週間以内であれば料金の50％、2週間を超える場合は全額を請求させていただきます。

貸出作品又は貸出作品データのチェック

原画、ポジ、作品データの管理には万全を期しておりますが、ご利用いただく場合は、お客様の方で作品の状態のチェック、作品データのウイルス、損壊等のチェックを必ず行って下さい。その際に問題がございましたらすぐにご連絡下さい。ご使用後（印刷入稿、ホームページ等の電子媒体へのデータアップも使用に含みます）のクレームは一切お受けいたしかねます。

肖像権その他

弊社では作品の中に含まれている人物、商品、場所、建物等に関する肖像権、商標権、著作権、特許権、意匠権、利用権に関してのトラブルが万一生じた場合、責任は負いかねます。お客様の責任において処理解決していただきます。

貸出作品のトリミング及び改変等

貸出作品のトリミング・変形・合成・切り抜き・改変等は著作権侵害となります。作品使用上、やむを得ないトリミング等の処理が必要な場合は著作権者の許諾を得るため弊社へ必ずお問い合わせください。

印刷物・掲載誌

作品をご使用いただいた場合は、印刷物及び掲載誌を2部必ずご提出下さい。ウェブサイトでのご使用の際は作品が使用されているページのURLを必ずご報告下さい。

不正及び無断使用

弊社の許可無く掲載作品を使用した場合、著作権侵害となり規定料金の3倍の料金を補償していただきます。なお補償金以上の損害が生じた場合（あるいは不正使用により補償金以上の利益を得た場合）には別途損害をお支払いいただきます。

第三者使用の禁止

貸出作品の使用許諾はお客様に限られ、貸出作品あるいはデータなどを第三者に使用させ、譲渡するなどはできません。第三者の使用などは無断使用となり、お客様と第三者に不正、無断使用による補償、損害をお支払いいただきます。

著作権侵害

作品の著作権、著作者人格権、所有権及び版権は全て作家に帰属します。本誌掲載の作品を参考に、無断で模写、リライト等をして印刷物その他に使用することは著作権及び著作者人格権を侵すことになり、問題が生じた場合はお客様の責任となります。

*asterisk